I0462562

Amazon.com

First published by Amazon/CreateSpace

ISBN-13: 978-1493692514
ISBN-10: 1493692518

Printed in the United States of America

This book is printed on acid-free and recycled products.

What Employers Want Most!

People Skills

By

Darrell Berkheimer

Amazon/CreateSpace

Contents

Prologue and Dedication

My first book – **Stories from The Golden Throne** – was produced to be a legacy, and to provide entertainment and thought for those who read it.

That book, published by **AuthorHouse**, is an anthology of 77 short items, most of them less than two full pages. Many were published by the daily newspapers where I had worked.

This book, however, was written for the best reason – to provide a service to people seeking to improve their lives.

It is designed especially to help young men and women compete in today's global situations. They need to make use of every tool and technique available – not just to excel, but often just to get good employment.

With soaring costs of health care and education, young parents must seek higher wages to provide for their needs and the needs of their children.

This book is dedicated to several friends and others for their support and encouragement.

Alan Johnson of Orem, Utah, provided moral support when it was needed most. Chuck Cole, who was a gifted teacher at Utah Technical College at Provo, compiled some of the included materials. And Phyllis Phillips of Provo, Utah, set an example for me to follow with her humor and attitude.

Three employees of Butte School District encouraged me to prepare the adult evening course on communications, which led to the idea for this book. They are: Chris Fisk, Kathy Cannon and Linda Baker.

More encouragement came from Rita Matheson, my companion and best friend, and the late Donna Larson of Butte, Montana – a grand lady of bubbling personality. Everyone needs a Donna Larson in their life to boost their ego.

For those curious about **The Golden Throne** moniker, an explanation is provided in the **Afterword**. There, too, is a free verse item, titled **Beauty and Life** and a **Mystery Philosopher** essay. All three are reprinted from my first book.

Darrell Berkheimer

1 - The Why!

Do you want people to listen to you?
Do you want to make more money?
Do you want to influence others?
Do you want to write better?
And do you want to speak better?
Do your words sometimes backfire on you?

If you have answered yes to any of those questions, then this book is for you – because it is designed to help you improve in each of those areas.

The purpose of this book is to draw attention to all of the aspects of people skills in a single source – with tips and guides to assist you in improving yourself.

But you will find little that is new or different in this book that you can't find elsewhere – but separately in various other books.

We have seen many technological developments in communications during the past 50 years. But the characteristics of people have not changed. This book concentrates on the people skills needed in communications rather than technology.

In discussing ideas for this book with a few young people, they admitted to reacting to an emphasis in recent years on gaining knowledge and technical skills, while training in people skills has received less attention.

So this book draws heavily on sources of 40 and 50 years ago. Those sources cited the need back then for more emphasis on interpersonal relations.

You can find more in-depth explanations of the concepts noted here in other books on writing, public speaking, psychology, leadership and management. This book, however, is designed to present those concepts with simplicity, and brevity, in an easy-to-grasp format.

It was developed as a result of two projects, with some of the information originally gathered for a daylong communications seminar. In 2012, those basic materials were expanded for an adult continuing education course at Butte School District in Montana.

The course was titled: **"Improving Communications – Through Writing, Speaking and Photography."**

The seminar materials were gathered in Provo, Utah, in the 1980s – with Charles "Chuck" Cole, a former instructor at Utah Technical College at Provo. Much has been added to those materials as a result of more recent articles and reports.

Although there are many tips throughout this book to improve your life through people skills, the **most powerful 4-letter word** in the English language is the **Number One Tip.**

That word is **READ**. And that word is emphasized repeatedly throughout this book.

- **Reading will improve your speech.**
- **Reading will improve your writing.**
- **Reading will improve your income.**

And by improving your speech, your writing, and your income, reading will improve your life.

Reading is a principle source of learning – second only to observation. Raymond Schuessler – in an article titled "Why Executives Fail" – wrote: "When you stop learning, you'll stop succeeding."

So one of the first books you should read – after this one – is Dale Carnegie's *"How to Win Friends and Influence People."*

2

That book – first published in 1936 – became an overnight success. It sold more than a million copies in less than a year, and was printed abroad in 14 languages. For 10 years, it stayed on *The New York Times* best-seller list. My copy is a 1964 edition.

Carnegie's book resulted from a YMCA course that he began teaching in 1912. Others are still teaching that course today – because the principles remain as important and applicable as they were 100 years ago.

I believe those ideas and principles are even more important today – especially for young adults. Because today – with an increasing population and global economy – our young workers face continually increasing competition – just to get a good job.

"Do Your Words Backfire?" is the title of a speech that I gave when I was a member of a Toastmasters chapter at Provo, Utah, where I was elected president of that group. That speech is reprinted at the end of this chapter.

A copy of that speech is one of many guides and checklists that were distributed as a part of the Improving Communications course. Many of those items will be included and added to the chapters of this book.

This book emphasizes reading and the development of good writing first – because they foster serious thought in all communications.

Good writing and good speaking <u>require considerable thought</u> – plus that other important 4-letter word – **WORK**.

You likely have heard the comment: "Engage mind before speaking." It's more natural to do that when writing – because we know that writing can provide a permanent record. What is written is not as fleeting as what we say in speaking.

That is why the more writing we do, the better our speech becomes. Because writing forces us to develop the habit of thinking about the words we choose to use. And that habit will carry over into our speech.

About Motivation

There are no shortcuts to good writing and good speech. They require WORK – lots of practice.

Good writing and good speaking require knowing your subject well. And that requires research that involves reading, interviewing, and taking extensive notes.

So a bit about motivation is appropriate.

This book will not motivate you. Motivation must come from within you.

Speakers and writers might inspire you to consider what you might accomplish if you decide to act on those inspirations. Those speakers and writers might motivate you to take the first steps in a plan or project.

But the motivation to continue a project until its completion comes from within.

It is that continuing motivation that establishes good habits and prompts us to continue with those good habits – indefinitely.

When many of us were young, when we became infatuated – fell in lust, or love – and then married, many of us had the mistaken idea that we would change our partner – <u>after</u> we married.

Divorces were among the results.

With age, however, most of us learned there is only one person that we can change – ourselves. And the changes we make come as a result of the motivation within us.

As with nearly all learning in life – what you get out of this book will be directly proportional to the motivational effort you exert in applying its tips and guidelines.

As you read on, you will notice some repetition. But repetitions and practice are the work that is necessary to become good at whatever we do – just as it is the practice, practice, practice that creates the finest musicians.

Finally, this book has been designed to provide procedures, guidelines and sources to aid in improving communication abilities and people skills.

And thus, we return to emphasizing that most powerful 4-letter word – READ.

Reading and writing must come first – because they have such a significant bearing on critical thinking and decision-making.

But people skills are not just writing and speaking. So this book also examines non-verbal signals and other aspects. It is designed to emphasize the total communications we provide through group situations as well as personal, one-on-one interactions.

In retrospect, I wish a handbook like this had been available when I was a young man – because it took me a lifetime to learn some of its principles.

What follows is the Toastmasters speech mentioned earlier, plus copies of checklists provided during the communications course.

In some cases, the checklists repeat statements made in the text of each chapter. The lists were provided both for emphasis and conciseness while limiting the need for students to take notes.

Do Your Words Backfire?

A Toastmasters speech

I was reading a book the other day, and I came across this statement:

"Better to be silent and be thought a fool, than to speak and remove all doubt."

I thought that statement was quite appropriate to use in a talk about the need for us to build our language skills.

I also found a couple of interesting questions on the subject, too.

A professor asked: "What three words are used the most by college students?"

A student said: "I don't know."

"That's correct," the professor remarked.

Another student was asked if he had read the dictionary.

That student's smart-aleck reply was:
"No; I'll wait until they make it into a movie."

But did you know that a standard desk dictionary has nearly a half-million words in it, while the average person tries to get by with only about 2,000?

So just why is it essential that you improve your language skills?

Why should we increase or add to the variety and number of words we use?

Dale Carnegie, in his chapter on diction – the last chapter in his book on public speaking – notes that others judge us by the way we talk.

Carnegie explains we have four different contacts with other people, who evaluate us in those four categories.

We're evaluated by:

1. **What we do**; 2. **How we look**; 3. **What we say**; and 4. **How we say it**.

Notice that two of the four categories involve our speech.

That means half of our evaluations in life depend on how we speak and the words we use.

Having a good command of our language, then, can help give us an advantage when we apply for a job, seek a promotion, or request a raise in pay.

On the contrary, failure to use our language properly can create a disadvantage.

A recent survey noted the U.S. workforce is flooded with poorly educated workers – including managers and supervisors – who simply can't read, write or add well enough to perform basic tasks properly.

So, if you are well skilled in reading, writing – and yes, arithmetic, too – won't you have an advantage when seeking improvement in your status and income?

Carnegie, in the same chapter on diction, tells about an Englishman who had no job, almost no money, and was dressed in shabby clothes, yet was able to get a most desirable job with a top financial company – all because of his command of the English language.

Carnegie says: "His diction became an immediate passport into the best business circles."

Now let's consider how poor language skills can work against you.

How impressed are you when you hear people use words improperly?

When you hear someone say **they was** instead of **they were**? ... **I done** instead of **I did**? Or **I seen** instead of **I saw**?

How impressed are you when someone uses a "sound-alike" word improperly?

Comedian Norm Crosby became famous by using sound-alike words instead of the correct ones. That's called **malapropism**.

Recently, I received a letter from a teachers' organization. The letter stated the organization's interest in "providing an **excellant** education for the students" in the county. But the letter misspelled the word **excellent**.

And the letter was addressed to our Toastmaster chapter -- leaving the "s" off Toastmasters.

The letter suggested that if our chapter ever needed a program on the subject of education, the teachers' organization would be delighted to provide it.

Such a letter – with improper word usage – can and will backfire, raising questions about the competency of the organization and its members.

I found a related item in Zig Ziglar's book, titled "**See You at the Top**." It reported: "The International Paper Company has statistical evidence supporting the claim that the bigger a person's vocabulary, the bigger the income."

These examples should indicate to you why it is important to make continuing efforts to improve language skills – by using both the dictionary and the thesaurus.

In doing so, we will develop:

> ◼ *A pride and confidence in our language skills;*
> ◼ *An improved competitive position when seeking a better job or promotion;*

- ◢ Improved salesmanship for our ideas, services or products, and
- ■ Considerably more effectiveness in general communications.

Again, I recommend that you read Dale Carnegie's books. They present many more reasons why we should improve our language skills – with lots of good examples.

# # #

Reading Improves Both Writing & Speech

Thoughts and quotes from Dale Carnegie's book titled:

"How to Develop Self-Confidence and Influence People by Public Speaking"

What we say and how we say it – in both writing and speech – is how we affect other people the most.

Yet many people blunder through a long lifetime – after leaving school – without any conscious effort to enrich their use of words.

They use the overworked and exhausted phrases of the office and the street. Small wonder their talk lacks distinction and individuality.

"How little there is that is new! How much even the great speakers owe to their reading and to their association with books."

"Books! There is the secret! He who would enrich and enlarge his stock of words must soak and tan his mind in the vats of literature."

How to Build Language Skills

(By Dale Carnegie)

Your diction will reflect the company you keep.
So keep company with the masters of literature.
Read a portion of an <u>enduring</u> book each day ...
... even if it's only 20 pages.
Read with a dictionary by your side.
Study the derivation of the words you find and use.
Don't use shopworn, threadbare words. Be precise.
Select words that give the shade of meaning that you want.
Strive to say precisely what you mean – to express the
most delicate nuances of thought.
Don't use trite comparisons.
Strive not only to be exact, but to be fresh and original.
Create your own similes, metaphors and analogies.
Have the courage to be distinctive.

Goals for Good Communications

A former president of Toastmasters International – William D. Hamilton – summarized what he considered to be the goals for good communications.

1. To laugh, chuckle and smile often
2. To win the respect of intelligent people and the affection of children
3. To earn the appreciation of honest critics, and induce the betrayal of false friends
4. To appreciate beauty
5. To find the best in others
6. To leave the world a bit better – whether by a healthy child, a redeemed social condition, or a job well done
7. To know even one life has breathed easier because you live
8. This is to have achieved good communication.

The 7 Deadly Sins of Communication

(If you communicate items that are helpful, appropriate, and which foster understanding, you can effectively influence and inspire others.)

The Sins:

1. **Bad timing** (too early or too late)
2. **Indifference**

   If you want your message to be received, you must address the needs, wants and dreams of your audience.
3. **Hesitancy**

   You can't duck or ignore difficult situations and still be respected.
4. **Prejudice**

   People aren't interested in your problems; but they are vitally interested in their own.
5. **Smoke Screening**

   Pompous words only indicate pompous people.
   (Learn big words; then forget about them. It's only important that you know them.)
6. **Arrogance**

   A know-it-all attitude shows insecurity – a weakness masquerading as strength.
7. **Incompetence**

   We need both knowledge and skill to inform, inspire and persuade others.

   Be curious about people, places, things and ideas. Additional study, reading, observing, research, and experience will build your communication abilities.

   Skill requires the repetition of practice, practice, and more practice.

2 - The Why of Writing!

Just how important is writing?

Sylvia Porter wrote in her newspaper column of years ago – "Your Money's Worth" – that companies single out communication skills ahead of production, financial or marketing abilities as the executive talent they value most.

In addition, executives throughout business and government will tell you that writing is one of the most important skills an ambitious young person can have.

So the person who is able to write simply and clearly – in addition to having knowledge and experience in his or her field – is more likely to get the job of his or her choice, and to succeed quickly in that position.

Some people who shun writing – or are reluctant to write for whatever reason – often attempt to get by with talk instead.

Sometimes that works – for a while. But oral communication can cause problems and waste time, money and energy – when the writing of a note or memo would provide the clarity that's needed.

A friend once asked: "What do you expect to accomplish with your writing?

It caught me a bit by surprise; so I thought for a few moments before answering. Then I replied that if I simply motivate people to think about how a situation can be improved, then I will have accomplished something important.

I explained that the role of writers is to present the information, raise the important questions, and identify the alternatives. Many writers don't have any better answers than their readers.

Writers realize readers not only want to know about

events and situations, but – even more importantly – they want to know why, and the effects of those events on their lives.

Increasing Emphasis on Writing

We all know the United States has evolved from a Manufacturing-Industrial Society to an Informational-Services Society.

In manufacturing, communications were important – to explain to workers what they needed to accomplish. But communications then were not nearly as important as they are today in our Information Society – and in today's global competition.

In international operations, most jobs involve exchanges of ideas and concepts that require vastly more precise communications. Writing – with clarity – provides the preciseness that is demanded.

Writing helps eliminate problems with people in different countries using different languages.

Writing can spawn some obstacles, too. Among the greatest obstacles to good writing are false notions that people have!

Good writing should always have as its purpose the desire to communicate and inform as quickly and succinctly as possible.

Many writers, perhaps without conscious awareness, appear to work very hard – not to explain, persuade or entertain – but to impress. Instead, we must use writing simply to be of service.

Aspiring writers – and those preparing business reports – face two other major obstacles, which they create for themselves.

One results from a false notion that they need to set the stage for their report, rather than jumping into the meat of it. The other results from a failure to spend the necessary time needed for organization.

Organization can be simple if all thoughts are written into notes that can be grouped into categories.

Then it's only a matter of arranging the categories and notes into a flow that provides easy transitions from issue to issue, or incident to incident

If you are having a problem getting started in writing, pick a subject on which you have a passionate opinion and thoughts. Then combine that passion with appropriate research and knowledge. You might also consider applying the techniques outlined in Chapter 6 on Persuasion.

The Best Writing

What tends to impress readers the most – perhaps even without them realizing it – is the ease of reading that results from brevity, simplicity and good organization. Writing coaches and editors find it impossible to over-emphasize those three attributes.

Conclusions: The best writing offers quick comprehension. And readers like a fast-paced presentation.

One study on comprehension revealed readers tend to have 100 percent comprehension of a 12-word sentence. That compares with 85 percent from a 17-word sentence – and <u>a decline to only 10 percent comprehension from a 43-word sentence</u>.

Long paragraphs also make reading more difficult and reduce comprehension.

Both long, compound-complex sentences and large blocks of black or gray type are intimidating to the reader's eye. They make reading more difficult and reduce understanding.

Shorter sentences and paragraphs, instead, tend to create feelings of immediacy, intimacy and drama.

Few people – including some professional writers – seem to grasp the importance of frequent paragraphing.

Readers in today's society have many desires and demands tugging at them for their time. And reader studies have concluded the easier – and more interesting – that you make it for the reader to devour your writing, the more your writing will be devoured.

Need for Eye Relief

Large blocks of type and long sentences cause readers to lose their place if they are even slightly interrupted. But shorter paragraphs of one to three sentences make it easy for them to return to where they were.

That is because the white space between paragraphs provides needed eye relief.

This is especially true when publishing restrictions do not allow for a full line of space between paragraphs – which provides the most desirable appearance for ease of reading.

Without that line of space, the partial empty lines at the end of paragraphs, and the indentations at the beginning of the next paragraphs provide eye relief.

Some publications – to make it easier on the reader – will provide an extra half-line of space between paragraphs. That is what this book provides.

Reader eye relief is just as important in writing as comic relief is necessary in good dramas. Both are designed to break mounting tension. And anything that makes it easier for the reader makes our writing more attractive.

Dialogue provides ease of reading. A major reason is the frequent paragraphing that results from switching from one speaker to another.

Poetry is another example. It's easy to read for the same reason – lots of white space.

And in varying the length of paragraphs, a short declarative sentence, standing alone – with extra space above and below it – can provide emphasis similar to a long pause in speech.

Boldface category headings also provide white space and ease of reading.

Importance of the Beginning

In today's markets, fiction writers are advised that they need to have fast-paced narratives with engaging characters.

But no matter how good someone's writing might be, that effort could be wasted if the writer fails to grab the attention of the reader at the very beginning.

Often, the quick, short "punch" of information is a good way to begin.

Louis L'Amour was one writer whose beginnings offer excellent examples of how to draw in the reader. He wrote more than 100 novels; and several hundred million copies were sold.

One reason for his success was his ability to grab and hold the reader's attention from the very beginning. And he often did it with dialogue in the first paragraph.

The beginning – whether in writing or speaking – should be one or two crisp sentences that make immediate sense.

Here are some examples that I used at the beginning of several articles in my previous book, **Stories from The**

Golden Throne. Three of the four were used to begin weekly columns published by the newspapers where I had worked.

- *"Generally, banana cream pies are among my favorite pastries. But not the one I had Saturday night."*

- *"His death came a month shy of his 15th birthday. That was less than three weeks ago, and the lingering feelings now are more of guilt rather than grieving."*

- *"Some people might have referred to him as a bum, or a drunk – as some of his actions and statements indicated. But he deserved no less respect than any other person; so I listened."*

- *"Grand Teton National Park has provided me with an attitude adjustment."*

Notice how each of these examples raises questions designed to draw the reader into reading further to learn the answers. Readers want to know the answers to why – or how.

Aspiring writers tend to get involved in "setting the stage" rather than jumping right into the meat of the story or the conclusion of the report.

Many folks learned – back in high school – that writers need to provide answers to the all-important questions of **who, what, where, when and why.** In addition, journalism instructors might add **how, and how much.**

But all of those questions do not need to be answered immediately.

Of course, when writing for an employer, your supervisor likely will expect you to begin with **"the bottom line,"** and then provide reasons or facts to substantiate your conclusions. That supervisor also will expect brevity.

Good writers – if they have the time – will rewrite and revise their beginning numerous times before they settle on something that satisfies them.

Even daily media writers, facing a deadline in a half-hour, may spend the first five minutes or more of that valuable time on just the beginning.

The Role of Purpose

A few writers have been able to get away with extensive "stage setting" – because of the acclaim they have received for what comes after. One such writer is James Michener.

In many of his books, Michener starts with the beginning of time and creation as the reader struggles through the first 50 or 60 pages. But readers continue through that struggle because they have learned that the narrative takes a turn to excellence for the remainder of the 400 to 700 pages of his books.

Readers know that Michener's fiction is based on historical events, and that his fictional characters are well developed toward providing a great understanding of that history. That obviously is the purpose of his writing.

I'm not sure how many readers are aware of the points and purpose of the westerns written by Louis L'Amour – because so many of them appear to be written simply for fast reading and entertainment.

L'Amour has written that his novels are geographically and historically correct, with little deviation. But his novels also are quite philosophical – with emphasis on ethics, morality and chivalry.

In a speech presented at a Toastmasters meeting, I referred to L'Amour as my "Mystery Philosopher." That speech later became a newspaper column published shortly after his death when I was City Editor at *The Daily Times* at Farmington, N.M. That column is reprinted in this book's Afterword.

As L'Amour continued to write, I believe his purpose went well beyond writing books to entertain and make money. I believe his purpose included stating philosophical truisms and emphasizing the morality and ethics that should guide how we live our lives.

Beginning writers seem to have difficulty limiting themselves to the purpose or general theme of their story. They allow themselves to get sidetracked on unrelated events or issues, which become major distractions.

Compulsion to Write

One author indicated he writes more from compulsion than purpose.

Warner B. Bair II, the author of a mystery-thriller series, explained why writers of that genre tend to become so prolific.

He reported the main characters in his novels "live" within his mind. He noted that as he goes about his various activities, he will envision situations and events that spawn his desire to put his characters in those settings.

Because he has developed his characters so vividly in his mind, he foresees how his characters would react to various situations and stimuli. And he feels a compulsion to write about what his characters would do.

As he moves from one novel to the next, he sees his characters growing and developing more intricately as a result of their previous experiences in his stories. He says characters drive plot rather than the reverse.

Bair developed a somewhat unusual twist for his main character, who he never refers to by a given name. So his books with the anonymous character are referred to as the "Anon Series."

That creates some writing difficulties for Bair – when he needs to have other characters hailing his anonymous man.

Use Quotes with Discretion

For non-fiction and business writers – especially media journalists – I have a generous dose of advice on the use of quotes. We have all heard the following complaints:

- **"I was misquoted."**
- **"I didn't say it that way."**
- **"It was taken out of context."**

Unfortunately, too often those complaints are valid – all because a poorly trained writer failed to use some discretion.

News media writers, particularly, seem to think they need to have colorful quotes in order to have a good story. And seldom do print and broadcast editors give good instructions on how and when to use quotes.

They should be advised to use caution and be discerning.

The idea that frequent quotes are needed throughout a report often is wrong. What is more important is concise paraphrasing that quickly conveys the proper meaning and the points that the information source was trying to make.

There are only four reasons for using a quote. The first two apply to most occasions, while the last two are limited to special circumstances. They are:

- *When the quote states something so well that it can't be stated any better or more concise;*
- *When the quote provides a certain accurate and needed flavor or color to the story – which otherwise would be missing if it was not used.*
- *To highlight exchanges and testimony in trials, hearings, meetings and other garrulous encounters.*
- *For pertinence. Newsworthy speeches require considerable direct quotation. It's advisable to give significant passages in the speaker's own words, even if they lack sparkle.*

Many journalists, including some of the best writers and broadcasters, can't speak nearly as well as they can write. That's simply because writing provides more opportunity to think about grammar and which wording is best.

Because few of us can speak with excellent diction, we might use double negatives or poor sentence construction. We might even make some silly statement that seems almost opposite to the point we are trying to make.

That particular quote – by itself – when taken out of context, can make us sound ridiculous or nonsensical.

Common Sense and Respect

Poorly trained writers will seek out such glitches and highlight them in their reports. Is it any wonder we sometimes hear complaints such as the ones noted above?

Responsible writers concentrate on the objectives, issues and tone of the speaker. And when possible, they will repeat to the source their understanding of what was said to confirm the meaning.

21

When writers no longer are guilty of making slips of the tongue when speaking, only then will they have a right to be insensitive to the slips of others.

Brevity – a sensible report on the issues emphasized by the source – should be the writer's main objective.

Selecting quotes merely to be sensational, misleading or demeaning is unethical and irresponsible. Instead, common sense and respect should prevail.

Common sense and discretion also are needed in the use of profanity and slang.

The Need for Confirmation

One final tip: Good editors and supervisors do not like single-source articles or reports when controversial issues are involved.

They want additional sources to confirm controversial issues. And they usually expect to see contradictory views from other sources. Then the reporting is more objective rather than subjective.

Failure to seek contradictory views opens the door to criticisms of a slanted or one-sided report.

Single-source items should be reserved for "personality spotlights" – designed to feature the views and activities of a single person, and often presented with the question-and-answer format.

The guidelines on the pages that follow originally were prepared for students attending my communications course. These guidelines are particularly pertinent for those people who must write about their company's business.

The Benefits of Writing

1. Writing can provide accuracy.
The accuracy of the spoken word declines as the message is passed from one person to the next.

Any child who has played the game of gossip knows this is true.

2. Writing improves memory.
The average person loses 50 percent of what he or she hears immediately after hearing it.

Within 24 hours, the average person will forget another 25 percent. The mere act of taking notes improves mental retention.

3. Writing is precise and permanent.
Written messages allow us to maintain copies of our communications for use days, weeks, and years later.

Written communications also allow us to share our knowledge, ideas and concepts with posterity.

4. Writing improves thinking.
Good writing requires logic and discipline

5. Writing improves speaking.
It's been proven: The more you improve your writing, the more your speaking improves.

6. Writing saves time.
It should be obvious that good writing – when clear and easy to read – will speed comprehension by those who need to understand the information.

7. Writing improves your image.
It provides the image of professionalism.
Most people will prefer your service if you look good on paper.

(Consider: Who would you prefer to perform your heart surgery? Would you prefer the intern with minimal experience; or the surgeon who has performed a half-dozen successful heart transplants?)

Essentials of a Good Newsletter

A good newsletter need be only one side of one page. But it may be necessary to provide a longer one as members and employees request or need additional information.

Longer newsletters are much more appreciated – particularly by members in those organizations that meet only once a month or less. But for organizations that meet frequently, more attention should be given to brevity of the items.

Membership readers don't like wading through long, flowery reports. Remember, the objective is to convey information quickly, accurately, with a touch of humor and, most importantly, in an easily readable manner.

Newsletters should **not** be considered as an opportunity for someone to impress the readers or express personal opinions.

Good Newsletters Provide:

◢ *Recognition for those who perform well.*
>> Note the member or employee of the month
>> Cite awards and honors won by members

◢ *Calendar of events.*
>> List any coming events – including those sponsored by other organizations – which may be of general interest to the membership.

◢ *Reports on personnel changes.*
>> Report on new members or new employees
>> Include reports on promotions or new jobs
>> Give new address on someone who's leaving

◢ *News of general interest.*
>> New policies and procedures – Most important
>> Births, deaths, birthdays and anniversaries
>> Tell changes coming soon, such as new equipment
>> Report accidents and member tragedies

◢ *At least one humorous item in each issue*

◢ *But be sure it is news.*
>> Don't use an item 2 months old or so stale that everyone already had knowledge of it 3 weeks ago.

Ten Commandments of Good Writing

These 10 rules can help you write so people will read and understand you.

1. Keep Sentences Short.
> *Use one thought per sentence. Keep relationships simple.*
> *Others understand better.*

2. Prefer the Simple to the Complex.
> *Simple expressions will make more sense.*

3. Avoid unnecessary words.
> *Don't be wordy.*
> *Avoid using redundant phrases.*
> *Use precise words.*

4. Prefer the Familiar Word.
> *Use words that communicate your meaning.*
> *Don't be a show-off with your vocabulary.*

5. Write as You Talk. –
> *This is good advice for getting your message across.*
> *Vocalize your writing – under your breath, in a whisper, or even out loud. If it sounds easily understandable when you vocalize it, then maybe it will be quickly understood by the readers.*
> *It may need a bit of polishing, but stick to this idea.*

6. Use Terms Your Readers Can Picture.
> *Abstract ideas need expression through mind pictures.*

7. Make Your Writing Relate to Your Readers.
> *Write to match the background and experience of your intended audience or readers.*

8. Write to Express – Not to Impress.
> *What good is your Ph.D. if your readers can't understand what you have written?*

9. Put Action into Your Verbs.
> *Passive tense fails to get results.*

10. Make Full Use of Variety.
> *Vary the length of sentences, paragraphs and style.*
> *Sometimes even slang is appropriate.*

When Writing Articles and Reports

1. **Grab the reader's attention with the beginning.**
2. **Come on strong.**
   - Use active, convincing words and phrases.
   - Be positive, not negative.
3. **Don't scare or intimidate the reader.**
   - With too many pages
   - Or with long sentences and paragraphs
4. **Ease into bad news**
5. **Be discreet**
   - You never know who might read what you have written.
   - And what you've written provides a record for frequent reference
6. **Be correct: With grammar, names, and titles.**
7. **Don't be lazy.**
   - Use the thesaurus. Search for the best word.
   - Use the dictionary. Verify spellings and definitions.
8. **Know the subject. Be sure of your "facts."**
   - When in doubt, check and confirm.
   - Conclusions are open to debate. Facts are indisputable.
9. **Avoid abbreviations and initials.**
   - Don't make your reader search for the meaning of those initials.
10. **Don't use etc., and avoid repeating favorite words.**
11. **Don't be flowery and pompous with inflated words.**
    - Use only as many words as you need, and no more.
12. **Be Clear.**
13. **Use words to suit your readers.**
    - Use technical terms ONLY when all your readers – ALL -- know their meanings.
    - Otherwise, you must adequately EXPLAIN their meanings.

14. **Be sure the reader knows who said what. (Attribution)**
    - And the use of too many "he's" or "she's" can be confusing
15. **Don't raise more questions than you answer.**
16. **Don't be cute.**
17. **Be modest.**
18. **Be neat.**
19. **End on a positive note.**
20. **Reread, edit and revise as often as necessary.**
    - <u>Until you are proud of it</u>

A Description of Good Writers

1. Good Writers know the purpose of their writing before they start.
2. Good Writers proofread their work.
3. Good Writers edit and revise their work
4. Good Writers spend more time on their writing than do poor writers.

3 - Public Speaking

A tiny book – with medium-size type, well-spaced lines, and published in 1935 with only 111 pages – is the best source you can get to prepare yourself for public speaking.

(Again, <u>READ</u> is the most powerful 4-letter word in the English language.)

That tiny book was used as the textbook for YMCA courses on public speaking back in the 1940s. That book is out of print, but it is still being used in classes on public speaking.

It's an excellent example of the statement that the size of the book has nothing to do with its significance. That little book on speaking is titled: ***"Public Speaking as Listeners Like it"*** – <u>by Richard C. Borden.</u>

Michael Buschmohle, a communications trainer at Sammamish, WA, wrote that Borden's book "is so clear and simple that his ideas stick like Velcro. They have stuck with me and I have used them for more than 40 years teaching presentation skills in 7 countries."

"Here's an example of his style," Buschmohle continued:

"Don't open your speech on Safety First by saying:
    'The subject which has been assigned to me is the reduction of traffic accidents.'

"Say, instead:
    'Four hundred and fifty shiny new coffins were delivered to this city last Thursday.'"

In 2010 Buschmohle wrote: "Borden's direct heart-to-heart advice is more valuable (today) than it ever was."

So both Borden and Buschmohle echo the observation that the beginning – in speaking as well as in writing – is all-important to draw the attention of your audience or readers.

Borden details his formula for speaking in four short chapters – on organization, substance, phraseology and delivery.

Isn't it somewhat amazing how the advice and instruction in both Borden's and Dale Carnegie's books on public speaking remain the focus of courses still being offered today – more than 70 years later?

I acquired Borden's book quite by accident. My father had the book because he attended one of the YMCA courses on public speaking.

I can't remember if he gave it to me, or if I found it among the books that he had. Nor can I remember if I got it before or after I bought two other books to assist me in speaking before a group.

The one is titled: ***"The Public Speaker's Treasure Chest"*** – by Herbert V. Prochnow and Herbert V. Prochnow Jr.

The other is ***"5000 One and Two Liners ..."*** – by Leopold Fechtner.

The Prochnows' book presents two chapters on how to prepare a speech, and how to make it sparkle. The rest of the book provides more than 4600 examples of witticisms, epigrams, similes, jokes, proverbs, colorful phrases, amusing definitions, quotations and anecdotes. Some, however, have become trite.

The first chapter begins by citing Cicero's emphasis on preparation and his five essentials of public speaking:

◢ *Choosing what to say;*
◢ *Arranging the material;*

- *Selecting well-chosen words;*
- *Fixing the speech in mind, and*
- *Delivering it with dignity and grace.*

The Prochnows note the two parts of a speech that are most difficult to prepare are the beginning and end. They advise agonizing over both to develop them well.

They also advise writing the speech in full after it is outlined. A pastor is quoted as saying he will spend as much as a half-hour preparing for each minute of his sermon.

Their book also notes that a speaker who is willing to tell a humorous story about himself provides a special joy for his audience.

The father-and-son book provides this four-point list for the body of the speech:

- *Know the subject thoroughly;*
- *Use facts, figures, and illustrations;*
- *If the audience is to be convinced of a proposal, begin with subject matter on which there is agreement, and*
- *Do not argue, but explain.*

Borden cites a simple two-word formula for the body of the speech – "so potent that it applies to the body of all speeches."

He says: "So magic are the words in this formula, that if you repeat them about once every ten sentences, the body of every speech you make must be interesting."

Those two words are: ***"For instance."***

Borden added that listeners not only like "for instances," but they demand them – and they want them in story form.

Attached are copies of a **Guide for Writing and speaking**, plus four checklists that were given to students in my course on improving communications.

The checklists are:

- *Borden's Format for the Formal Platform Speech;*
- *The Need for Self Confidence and Self-Esteem;*
- *10 Commandments for Public Speaking, and*
- *Designing the Presentation for Listeners.*

A Guide for Writing and Speaking

A "Key Words Technique" can make both speaking and writing easy.

I originally wrote these guidelines to train beginning reporters in how to quickly organize information when writing their stories.

But the process can easily be applied to organizing a set of notes into a coherent speech as well.

The process is simple.

The most complicated part is taking extensive notes – whether doing an interview, listening to a speaker, attending a meeting, or simply gathering information on line or at the library.

By taking extensive notes, the mere act of writing the information helps to impress it upon your mind.

When taking notes at an event, if you are worried that you might not have heard something correctly – such as an important number – immediately put a couple large questions marks in the left margin of your notes. They will serve as a "red flag" to remind you to double-check the number, the correct spelling of a name, or whatever other item requires confirming.

At a meeting or speech, those question marks will help you check the information immediately after – before the source leaves. This can save a lot of time later when you might have difficulty contacting that source.

When starting to write the article – or preparing the speech – simply read through your notes, circling a "key word" – or a short two- to three-word phrase – which will bring to your mind a particular point or series of items that should be included in your speech or story.

Number the Importance

Then list those key words on a sheet of paper in the order that they appear in your notes.

Next, number that list of key words in what you consider their order of importance. Keep in mind that some items of lesser importance might serve best in providing transitions from one major item to another.

Do not throw away the original list. It shows the order of the key words in your notes. That list makes it easy for you to locate and check details.

Finally, make a new list and number them again to provide an easy- or natural-flow sequence for the important issues of your article or speech.

This final numbering is the most important part of the key words technique, because it organizes your entire report or presentation.

Your final list should be the order in which you intend to refer to your key words as you speak or write the story.

If you have come to know the subject well – and the key word subjects are fresh in your mind – you likely will realize those key words are all you need in front of you to give the entire speech or write the entire story.

On many occasions, I have been able to write lengthy stories quickly by simply looking at my key words list.

But I kept my extensive notes handy so that I could check any details. That's when your first key words list –

showing their sequence in your notes – helps you quickly find a number, spelling or whatever you need to verify.

Occasionally I decided to quickly re-arrange the order of importance of the key words when I felt the article was not flowing as nicely as I thought it should. And you can do something similar in your mind when preparing and practicing your speech.

Since most of my writing has been for newspapers, many of my articles were not as long as full-blown magazine stories. But I have written enough longer articles and series to know that the same key words technique works just as well.

A longer article simply will take more time and probably require more checking of original notes to confirm details.

This technique has proven better and faster for me than any other. And when working on the production of a daily newspaper, speed is nearly as important as accuracy and quality.

Daily newspaper workers can ill afford to lose minutes – let alone larger chunks of time.

In speaking, I have found the key words process the quickest way to organize my presentation. In addition, I was able to do a better job of giving a speech by spending less time looking at notes and more time looking at the audience.

But beware of selecting too many key words. It is less likely that you will select too few; but if you mark too many your list may become too unwieldy.

From one key word, I've written as few as two sentences. But frequently one key word prompted me to write two or three paragraphs; and on some occasions a single key word or phrase sparked me to write an entire page.

The same is true in speaking. One key word could prompt several minutes of speech.

The better you know your subject – or the information linked to a particular key word or short phrase – the more you are able to recall and speak from one word or phrase.

In the writing, frequently I have spent almost as much time writing and rewriting the first three to five paragraphs as I did writing the entire rest of the story.

This is because the "lead" or beginning is all-important in both writing and speech.

No matter how excellent other parts of the article or presentation may be, you risk the possibility of "turning off" your readers or listeners if you do not have a beginning that attracts their attention.

If you are writing an article that you hope to sell, you had better have a beginning that attracts the attention of the editor or publisher, or you have wasted your time.

Regarding the use of a tape recorder, I've found they usually waste my time – unless a word-for-word, question-and-answer article is planned. Otherwise, I waste too much time hunting details as I zip back and forth on the tape.

If you are concerned about obtaining flawless quotes, use a tape recorder in addition to taking extensive notes. Then the sequence of the key words from your notes helps you locate what you need from the recording.

In the presentation – whether writing or speaking – vary the length of your sentences. But short, simple declarative statements will have the most effect.

Formal Speech Format

condensed from the book

Public Speaking as Listeners Like It

By Richard C. Borden – Copyright 1935

Ho Hum – *Light a Fire*

Your speech is not well organized unless you kindle a quick flame of spontaneous interest with your first sentence. (The same as with writing.)

Why Bring That Up? – *Build a Bridge*

Your listener lives on an island – an island of HIS interests.

You must <u>immediately</u> maintain the listener's attention by noting why this issue is important and how it affects the listener.

For Instance! – *Illustrate*
Listeners like for instances
- *In story form*
- *That involve famous people*
- *That animate the pages of history*
- *That are based on colorful analogies*
- *That are interwoven with visual aids*
- *That dramatize important statistics*

So What? – *Emphasize Your Point*
- *Ask for Action*
- *Tell What Is Needed*

Self-Confidence and Self-Esteem

Symptoms of Poor Self-Image
- Highly critical of others.
- Feels compelled to get recognition – even when not deserved.
- Bossy, unable to accept criticism.
- Feels threatened by confident people. ... Seeks to show them up.
- Will commit to do something, knowing it probably won't get done.
- Runs himself down, using self-critical statements such as:
  - "I blew it again."
  - "I knew I couldn't do it."

Building Self-Confidence & Self-Esteem
- Visualize and tenaciously hold a mental picture of yourself succeeding.
  - Your mind will seek to develop this picture. Never let it fade.
  - Never think of yourself as failing.
  - Never doubt the reality of the mental image
  - The mind always tries to complete what it pictures. So picture success.
- Deliberately voice a positive thought to cancel any negative thought.
- Do not build obstacles in your imagination.
- Get a competent counselor to help you understand your actions.
- Make a true estimate of your own ability, then raise it 10 percent.
- Do the things you fear to do and record in writing each success.

Help Another Person Build Self-Image
- *Point out their strong points.*
- *Cite their successes.*
- *Help identify ways to eliminate weaknesses.*

Confidence, Security and Knowledge come ...
from <u>Reading</u>, Listening and Observing

10 Commandments for Public Speaking

1. **Make the Right Speech in the Right Place.**
2. **Make your Opening Effective**
3. **Use a Positive Approach**
    Negativity turns off most people.
4. **Prepare Thoroughly and Practice, Practice, Practice**
    Rehearse often, and to anyone available.
    Your audience is expecting a good speech – so give one.
5. **Look Decent --** How you present yourself affects how well your audience will listen.
6. **Be Explicit and Factual**
    Don't be vague.
    Self-confidence comes from thorough preparation and subject knowledge.
7. **Use Voice Variations, Gestures and Pauses**
8. **Speak as if Talking to One Person**
9. **Don't Wander**
    Zero in. Don't try to cover too vast an area.
10. **Summarize**

Designing the Presentation for Listeners

(From Borden's book)

Listeners like speech phraseology that:
- Is Sincere;
- Free from verbal bloat and triteness;
- Grammatically sure-footed;
- Provides good transitions;
- Is Specific;
- Is Picturesque, <u>and most of all</u>
- Is CLEAR

4 - Personal Relations

A recent CNN Money article reported employers have difficulty finding candidates who can research, write, think creatively, and who also have interpersonal skills.

A good source to develop those skills is Dale Carnegie's book *"How to Win Friends and Influence People."*

If I accomplish nothing more from this book than prompting people to read Carnegie's book, then my effort in writing this book was a success.

Carnegie's book should be considered a manual for people skills.

So again, I must emphasize that most powerful 4-letter word in our language – <u>READ</u>.

Unfortunately, our public education system and religious organizations spend too much time teaching us to memorize and blindly follow rather than to THINK and QUESTION.

Instead, they should emphasize reading authors with opposing views. That is what fosters questioning and thinking.

Reading Dale Carnegie's book, however, will emphasize the importance of people skills.

Carnegie wrote that millionaire industrialist John D. Rockefeller once said: "... I will pay more for that ability than for any other under the sun."

To anyone seeking advancement to executive positions, people skills in Interpersonal Relations are the most important skills they can develop.

That's according to John J. Franco, who served as president of Xerox Learning Systems. He offered a system known as Advanced Executive Learning Skills.

That program continues to be offered by the American Management Association.

Franco wrote:

"The critical factor which determines an executive's success is the executive's ability to deal with people."

But it isn't just executives and managers who need people skills. Because good customer service abilities are among the most in-demand skills.

Nothing seems to irk people more than getting little or no satisfaction from customer service personnel.

Good customer service workers are hard to keep – because the work is so frustrating. Few companies realize the need to pay enough to keep the good ones.

The best customer workers will seek and "graduate" to better pay and more emotionally rewarding work – either within the company or with another.

Throughout his book, Carnegie reports how people skills will help everyone in their daily lives. My copy is riddled with under-linings throughout its six parts. Those six sections are:

1. *Fundamental Techniques in Handling People*
2. *Six Ways to Make People Like You*
3. *Twelve Ways to Win people to Your Way of Thinking*
4. *Nine Ways to Change People Without Giving Offense or Arousing Resentment*
5. *Letters That Produce Miraculous Results*
6. *Seven Rules for Making Your Home Life Happier.*

Here are just a few of the principles and conclusions noted in the book. The quotation marks indicate the exact wording in the book.

As we emphasize the need for education, too many young folks get the idea that education and knowledge alone will lead them to financial and professional rewards. Unfortunately, that just is not true.

"The ability to speak is a shortcut to distinction. ... And the man who can speak acceptably is usually given credit for an ability out of all proportion to what he really possesses."

"The way to develop self-confidence is to do the thing you fear to do, and get a record of successful experiences behind you."

Employees seeking promotions and advancement also need to develop another characteristic, which, in turn, helps to build confidence. It is the desire and ability to make others smile and chuckle when they see you.

One lady, who became adept at customer relations, told me she had to train herself to smile at every person she met. She added that it improved her attitude as well.

It is impossible to smile and make someone feel better and not feel better yourself.

Carnegie cited a shop owner's listing of the value of a smile.

It costs nothing, but creates much.
It enriches those who receive, without impoverishing those who gave.
It happens in a flash and the memory of it sometimes lasts forever.
None are so rich they can get along without it, and none so poor but are richer for its benefits.
It creates happiness in the home, fosters good will in a business, and is the countersign of friends.
It is rest to the weary, daylight to the discouraged, sunshine to the sad, and Nature's best antidote for trouble.
Yet it cannot be bought, begged, borrowed, or stolen, for it is something that is no earthly good to anybody till it is given away!

Successful leaders have realized they need to develop the art of making little quips or comments to prompt others to smile and chuckle.

I recall one news reporter I worked with who later was selected to be managing editor. He had that ability and used it well.

On one occasion, when the two of us went out to lunch, we saw two attorneys who we knew, who were taking a break from courthouse duties. My reporter friend smiled and said: "Hi, handsome and ugly."

We all chuckled over that briefly as each of us wondered: Which one was he calling handsome and which was the other?

And my reporter friend was smart enough to quickly change the subject by asking about something that was happening at the courthouse that day.

I must add that he got the job that I had coveted back then. In fact, I had been his local news editor, who spent time training him.

I was more knowledgeable technically; but he had the better people skills. And it took me years to admit that he was better prepared for the job – that his people skills were more important than my technical and mechanical skills.

Carnegie emphasizes the importance of caring about others and being sensitive to their problems. And his advice on criticism is especially important in relations with others. He advises talking about your own mistakes before criticizing others.

His book states:

"Criticism is futile because it puts a man on the defensive, and usually makes him strive to justify himself. Criticism is dangerous because it wounds a man's pride, hurts his sense of importance, and arouses his resentment."

A couple pages later, he adds:

"Let's realize that criticisms are like homing pigeons. They always return home. Let's realize that the person we are going to correct and condemn will probably justify himself, and condemn us in return."

Three other publications that offer exceptionally good advice on People Skills are booklets that were prepared for the Jaycees organization. They are titled **Personal Dynamics, Communication Dynamics,** and **Leadership Dynamics.**

Each of the booklets is a short project course with lists, guidelines and procedures for the project participant to improve his abilities in those areas. They are excellent personal growth manuals.

Personal Dynamics is a particularly good project course for any young adult who seems to lack direction. It details a process for establishing goals, and then lists procedures for achieving those goals.

The skills needed in Interpersonal Relationships are listed in Chapter 4 of that booklet. They are:

- *Make the other person feel important*
- *Care about the other person's problems*
- *Always be fair and honest in your dealings*
- *Be considerate of the other person's time*

One of the concepts inspirational speakers explain is the difference between being reactive and pro-active.

We humans have a tendency to bristle in a somewhat defensive or aggressive manner when confronted with anything we consider a bit offensive or disagreeable – such as criticism. We tend to react defensively – often when we simply misunderstood something that was said.

Speakers on Interpersonal Communications dwell on the difference between being reactive and pro-active.

42

They cite our tendency to react immediately in a negative way – without thinking – and how doing so can create difficulties and problems.

They explain the solution to avoid those problems is simple – stop to <u>think before responding</u>. Then we can choose what we consider is the best way to respond.

To do that consistently, we must develop the habit of pausing in silence whenever we think we are being criticized or attacked in some way.

Skepticism Is Healthy

Most of us have a tendency to be too accepting of what we heard or saw. That's when a healthy dose of skepticism becomes important.

That skepticism is important especially when we hear rumors about others.

The best print and broadcast media managers are diligent about training reporters to be skeptics – to guard against immediate acceptance and judgment of what they read or heard.

Good media managers issue strong warnings against repeating unconfirmed or unjustified statements – especially because of the potential legal ramifications.

And skepticism is important particularly when an expert or authority in one field is commenting on another area not related to his or her area of expertise.

The thinking and questioning – which comes from reading different views – also can yield a skepticism that helps us pause before jumping to errant conclusions.

<u>We need to apply that same skepticism to our judgments in first impressions</u>.

All too often first impressions of other people are wrong, which we usually come to realize as a result of later meetings. So it is wise to be a skeptic about your first impressions of others.

The Jaycees **Communication Dynamics** booklet states:

"It takes some degree of maturity to be an effective communicator – maturity to:

- **Withhold judgment,**

- **Avoid jumping to conclusions, and**

- **Accept another person's feelings and not get upset because of the way they feel."**

Our tendency to judge another person's feelings is among the biggest killers of communication," the booklet says.

It adds that a creative-mature person is someone who is flexible, open-minded, sensitive, realistic, expressive about real feelings, curious, and self-accepting.

That booklet consists of four short chapters that examine:

- **The problems that occur in the communications process;**

- **The importance of listening;**

- **The human aspects of communications, and**

- **Reading and Writing – the two major parts of communication.**

Remembering Names

Carnegie tells a story about a boy, 10 years old, who lost his father in a freak horse incident. That boy never saw the inside of a high school.

But later, before he was 46, he received degrees from four colleges, became chairman of the Democratic National Party and U.S. Postmaster General.

When chatting with Carnegie about the secret of his success, Carnegie said: "I understand you can call ten thousand people by their first name."

That man replied: "No, you are wrong. I can call fifty thousand people by their first names."

Carnegie observed: "That ability (by that Democratic politician) helped put Franklin D. Roosevelt in the White House."

The "ability to remember names is almost as important in business and in social contacts as it is in politics," Carnegie adds.

He indicates that most people don't remember names simply because they fail to make it a priority. They just don't take the time and energy to concentrate and repeat names in an effort to fix them in their minds. Instead, they make excuses.

But he concludes that remembering a man's name **"is to him the sweetest and most important sound in any language."**

Listening

A failure to listen properly is the number one barrier to communications. A total of 10 are listed in a guideline added at the end of this chapter.

Raquel Welch said: "You can't fake listening. It shows."

And various sources advise: If you wish to be a good conversationalist, try active listening.

One study noted we can speak at 150 words per minute, but our minds whiz along as fast as 800 or more words per minute. So listening takes active concentration.

The Jaycees booklet on **Communication Dynamics** advises that good listening does not come natural. It is a skill that must be developed. When you need to know more from someone, you will need to listen intently as that person speaks.

That booklet adds:

"A technique used by some people is to assume that every person has something worthwhile to say. When you take this approach to conversation, it becomes important that you hear all of the message in order to pick out the 'worthwhile' part.

"Develop in yourself a desire, a need to become a better listener, and your interest in other people will increase.

"A good listener is a hunter. He doesn't just sit back and wait for the message to 'happen' to him; he seeks it out."

The "Bottom Line"

Eventually, nearly everyone comes to realize it's not what you have, or what you can do that matters. It's the type of person you are that makes the difference.

What follows are several people skills' guides.

46

Body Language

As much as 80 percent of what we communicate is nonverbal.

That's according to former FBI agent Joe Navarro, who has become a nonverbal communications expert. He has written the book ***What Every Body Is Saying.***

That means every gesture – mouth twitch, raising eyebrow, and the way we stand can send a message. And researchers have been studying the science of body language for decades in efforts to help us communicate more effectively.

A UCLA professor emeritus of psychology, author of the book ***Silent Messages,*** says we relate to people in 3 ways – **verbally** (with words), **vocally** (tone of voice), and **visually** (body language). It's **"the 3 V's."**

That professor – Dr. Albert Mehrabian -- claims that we obtain more information from voice tone and body language than we do from a person's words. He says our facial expressions are the most important.

A psychologist, Dr. Paul Ekman, reports it's often quite difficult to even notice many revealing expressions because some flash by in a mere fraction of a second. Dr. Ekman, co-author of ***What the Face Reveals,*** is noted as a pioneer researcher in what he calls micro expressions.

Another author – an anthropologist – said the best salesman, the best teachers, the best business managers and most successful lawyers have one thing in common – the ability to understand nonverbal signals, and use them to their advantage.

David Givens, author of a book on the nonverbal communications, titled ***Love Signals,*** noted the most successful trial lawyers will look at a jury and judge and notice little cues that indicate what they are thinking.

He added that often an expression or movement signals a person's true feelings, which may be contrary to what is being said. He cites such actions as compressed lips, shoulder movements, body angle, and even the way our feet are pointing, can give various signals – in addition to hand and arm actions.

Givens reported that when an employee is receiving praise from a supervisor, the employee's toes invariably will point inward – a sign of submission – while the boss will toe out – a sign of dominance.

Givens also said that much of early courtship consists of nonverbal actions. He said turning "the cold shoulder" is one of the most recognizable gestures in the animal kingdom.

Givens particularly warned that touching must be used carefully because of its strong emotional impact.

Barriers to Communications

Poor Listening

Ignoring conflicting information

Emotions

Conflicting Non-Verbal Signals

Prejudices

Hearing What We Expect to Hear

Evaluating the Source

Perceived Irrelevance

Stereotypes - (generalizations)

Multiple Meanings of words -
> (RUN has more than 30 meanings – as a noun and verb)

Ten Commandments of Good Listening

(By Keith Davis, Professor of Management, Arizona State Universiity)

1. Stop Talking
2. Put the talker at ease
3. Show that you want to listen
4. Remove distractions
5. Empathize with the person
6. Be patient
7. Hold your temper
8. Go easy on argument and criticism
9. Ask Questions
10. STOP TALKING

The average person loses 50 percent of what was heard almost immediately.

If you are like the average person, within 48 hours you will forget an additional 25 percent. That means that even when you pay close attention, you probably will remember only one-fourth of what was said to you only 2 days earlier.

But I believe it is possible to increase that percentage substantially by forcing ourselves to develop good listening habits. We should strive to become better than average.

Caring and Being Sensitive

Caring requires:

- Being alert to the feelings and attitudes of others.
- Recognizing the signals of non-verbal communication.
- Understanding the other person's viewpoint.
- Asking if you can help when you notice someone is downcast.
- Becoming an active listener – without attempting to interfere.
- Using silence effectively – without feeling compelled to talk.
- Refraining from offering gratuitous advice or platitudes.
- Displaying empathy by showing an understanding of how another feels.

A Friend in Toastmasters Wrote:

There is no trick that's quite so sick
As to cut the other guy down;
To use his name and fix it with shame,
And make him out as a clown.
You have the choice to use your voice
To lift the human race;
For after all, when you make people fall,
It's really you who falls on your face.
-- by Don Bishop

Body Feedback

If he or she:

It MAY indicate:

If he or she:	It MAY indicate:
Crosses arms tightly ...	Disgust, or anger
Continually tries to change subject ...	Lack of interest in your topic
Seems anxious to end conversation ...	Bored; not interested
Says: "I see ... Yes ... I understand" and nods head ...	Definitely interested
Keeps looking at something else as if it is beckoning ...	Has something else to do at that time
Shuffles feet and moves about a lot ...	Bored; anxious to leave
Yawns frequently; looks out window ...	Just not interested
Seems confused; asks unrelated questions ...	Failure to understand your message

5 - Getting That Job!

Good people skills are necessary to getting desirable employment. Job candidates must realize their communication behavior will influence the result of an interview.

One videotape study of initial employment interviews was reported years ago by National Business Employment Weekly. It revealed a major difference in the communication skills of successful and unsuccessful job contenders.

Candidates first were evaluated on the basis of their written applications. Then those that looked best on paper were invited to an initial interview.

But many who looked best on paper were deemed "no job match" in contrast to those who were invited back for a second meeting.

Unsuccessful candidates lacked effective face-to-face communication skills. Successful candidates, however, provided evidence of their abilities through oral communication. They were positive and displayed confidence. They shined because they revealed their people skills.

Employers want to know more than whether a candidate can and will do the job. Employers want to know if the candidate will "fit in" – if he or she is "temperamentally suited" to join the team.

The study revealed how good writing is necessary to open the first door, but that good speech and people skills are needed to get the job.

A more recent report, issued in 2012 by **Forbes** magazine, cites the top five personality traits sought most by employers. The report observed that employers look for those five traits to determine if the applicant is a "cultural fit."

The five traits were identified as a result of a survey of employers conducted by *Universum*, a Stockholm-based company. The Forbes article reported *Universum* "annually surveys over 400,000 students and professionals on job-related issues."

The analysis listed the preferred personality traits by percentages. They are:

Professionalism (86%)

High-energy (78%)

Confidence (61%)

Self-monitoring (58%)

Intellectual curiosity (57%)

The task for applicants is to communicate – via their people skills -- that they have those traits.

Another Forbes article, published in December of 2012, listed **The 10 Skills That Will Get You Hired in 2013.** The top four of the 10 skills that were listed are:

-- *Critical Thinking;*

-- *Complex Problem Solving;*

-- *Judgment and Decision-Making, and*

-- *Active Listening.*

The rest of the 10 on the list relate to specific technical skills; so technical skills were considered of lesser importance to individual or personal skills.

The top three – *Critical Thinking, Problem Solving and Decision-Making* – can best be developed as a result of that most important 4-letter word in our language – READ!

Again, the task of candidates is to use their people skills to communicate that they have those traits.

The Forbes articles were among many recent ones dealing with job-hunting and networking – apparently spawned by the tough economy and high unemployment rates lingering throughout the nation as a result of the 2008-2009 Recession.

A few other excellent articles were published by **Inc.** magazine. Three were written by columnist Jeff Haden.

The one article identifies the 8 steps to a perfect job interview.

The 1st step – "Be likable" – is obvious, as Haden indicates. But he emphasizes that it's a critical step. He advises: "Be yourself, but be the best version of yourself you possibly can."

Step 2: "Never start the interview by saying you want the job." Haden adds: "Because you don't know yet."

His 3rd step is: "Ask questions about what really matters to you!"

For step 4, he says: "Set a hook." Haden then uses several sentences to basically tell the applicant to convey something distinctive about himself or herself, so he or she will be remembered.

In step 5, he advises the candidate must be prepared to state what he or she can offer immediately.

The 6th step also should be obvious: <u>Do not make negative comments</u>. If you haven't performed a particular task, explain that your training has prepared you to do so. That's the positive approach to saying, "I didn't do that."

For step 7, Haden advises: <u>Either ask for more information, or ask for the job</u>. But if you decide to ask for the job, you must be prepared to say why you want it, and why you should get it.

He concludes with an 8th step that also should be obvious – to <u>reinforce the connection with a follow-up contact</u>. On that, nothing is better than a hand-written note. And "never underestimate the power of gratitude," Haden says.

Another Haden article lists these five questions that every great job candidate should ask:

◤ *What do you expect me to accomplish in the first 60 to 90 days?*
◤ *What are the common attributes of your top performers?*
◤ *What are the few things that really drive results for the company?*
◤ *What do employees do in their spare time?*
◤ *How do you plan to deal with ...?*

With that last question, the candidate needs to decide in advance of the interview the one or two biggest challenges that the employer faces. Failing that, the candidate might ask: "<u>What is your toughest nut to crack, and how do you plan to deal with it?</u>"

Haden's articles include more detailed explanations, but both his lists emphasize opportunities for the candidate to show how he or she will fit into the employer's team. And that's exactly what I wanted to know when I was recruiting young reporters.

I realized I could be swamped with resumes from many places. And sifting through a resume stack can be time-consuming without revealing the information that's wanted.

I wanted to know how well the applicant questions and thinks. And I wanted to know if the applicant had a familiarity with the geographical area where he or she was applying to work.

Hiring someone from Minnesota or Illinois to work in west Texas – if they never even visited Texas – could result in cultural and geographic shock. That person could have trouble fitting in – establishing a prescription for quick turnover and staff instability.

I decided I needed to chat with an applicant to quickly get the answers I sought.

That's why, when placing an ad in the news media's magazine – *Editor & Publisher* – I simply listed a phone number and requested an applicant to call me.

In 10 to 15 minutes of chatting, I got the answers I sought and could then decide if I wanted the applicant to send a resume.

That procedure quickly narrowed the acceptable applicants to only a few. And in much less time I decided on the two best applicants to invite to a face-to-face interview.

I must add that I did hire one recent journalism graduate from Minnesota to fill a reporter's position at the *Big Spring Herald* in west Texas.

I hired her because she answered my questions well and because she graduated from college with a dual major in journalism and Spanish. She explained she definitely wanted to work in a border state so she could make use of her Spanish.

She communicated that she was the questioning and thinking reporter that I wanted.

(More than 25 years later, she still lives and works in Texas. She has worked at a couple of the best newspapers in the state, and as an editor of two major magazines.)

Finally, I must add an important tip about resumes:

Do not try to design a "one-size-fits-all" resume. Although it means additional work, a job applicant will enhance his or her chances of getting the job by revising or re-designing a resume for each job application submitted.

6 - The Personal Touch!

Everyone likes personal attention. And when they get it, they respond appropriately.

This is a personal relations skill that is so important it requires its own chapter.

Technology, computerization, robotic machines and outsourcing have combined to cause two major problems in the United States. They have eliminated jobs and reduced the personal touch.

The U.S. economy became stagnated by the loss of millions of well-paying middle-class and blue-collar jobs.

But some economists see the potential for a new middle class of workers – dubbed "new artisans" and composed of self-employed service workers and various technicians.

They will have problem-solving and vocational trade skills that can't be replaced by a computer. *But they also must be skilled in providing the personal touch whenever they face a competitive situation.*

Retail sales managers, service departments and small businesses with only two or three employees have known and preached the importance of the personal touch for many years. But much of that personal touch has been lost with the procedures offered through modern technology.

We have computer-generated responses by telephone; computer-generated replies by email, and – if we are lucky – we get a person in India, Pakistan or Vietnam, who we have difficulty understanding.

The younger generation has matured with that technology and situation while older workers have been forced to embrace it in order to remain competitive.

As a result, many workers in most fields now turn to email, voice mail, texting and web sites to conduct much of their business. And they have fallen into the trap of replacing the personal touch with those other avenues.

Modern technology acts like we are robots. We are treated like numbers, not people.

An article published by **Franchisee** asks: When was the last time you called a company and a person answered the phone?

And beyond that, when is the last time you got to talk to someone in the U.S.

Another article published by **Yahoo! Finance** reported managers in various offices have noticed two situations: Their offices have become unusually quiet; and sales are down.

One manager noted the members of her sales staff – all under 35 – were emailing clients with their pitches, not calling them on the phone.

One worker complained that she considers phone calls an interruption. Another reported he unplugs his desk phone and stashes it in a cabinet.

Such attitudes are indicative of lazy workers.

"Email won't cut it in professions like sales, where personal rapport matters," the sales manager remarked.

Another article published on the web site **WAHM.com** notes Internet offerings include:

- *Up-to-the-minute product selection on web pages;*
- *Auto-responders to act on requests;*
- *Immediate payment methods;*
- *Secure financial sites, and*
- *All sorts of e-tools.*

Then the article asks: So what is wrong?

You have a decent product and prices, but you're not being overwhelmed with sales, and barely making expenses. So why aren't they buying?

Then that article suggests: "Possibly they have questions that are not being answered, and would like to talk to a human being."

"And here is the funny part," the article continues; "they may not even want to talk with someone, but may just want to be sure there is someone to contact if there is a problem."

The article concludes that when businesses fail to provide proper contact information, including a means of talking to someone who can answer questions, then they can expect to lose potential customers.

But it's not just the sales department that needs to provide the personal touch. Auto dealers have known for years that their sales can vary in direct proportion to how well the service department is satisfying customers.

Personal-touch service is what provides return customers to plumbers, electricians, contractors, welders, installers, and various home and office repair services. They are the people deemed to be our modern middle-class.

That category also will include entrepreneurs who will learn that initiating a new project or product usually requires intensive personal touch and rapport.

The importance of personal touch is evident when we consider why we continue to deal with the same businesses year after year, or why we decided to switch to a different one. Most often the answer is because of the personal attention we received, or failed to receive.

One manager remarked: "All business essentially comes down to relationships." And that's true with the in-house staff as well external relationships.

A company recruiter said: "Many times, employees don't leave companies. They leave people." He explained that if supervisors don't provide appropriate personal treatment to workers, he will be kept busy working to replace those workers.

Managers and supervisors – and those who want to become supervisors – please take note!

Recruiters usually will be the first to report that retention is cheaper than recruiting, and that personal attention is what will retain experienced workers.

In the days of yesteryear, many older workers can recall that the best of their bosses maintained an open door policy. Issues could be resolved before they mushroomed into bigger problems – simply because the boss was accessible.

Personal touch can only be provided when the appropriate people make themselves available to give that personal attention.

I'm old-fashioned. I want a personal relationship with the owner of a local insurance agency where I can sit in his office and discuss issues – and maybe even personal activities. I don't want an insurance company that I must deal with only by phone, email or letters.

And I won't use ATM depositories. I want the people in the bank to know me personally – to say hello to me by using my first name or nickname.

Many people like that type of situation. The younger generations need to learn that when they establish the potential for similar one-on-one situations, they can both provide better service and receive better service.

One particularly good example of personal attention occurred when two of us visited a steak house. Either the owner or his son, who were both there that evening, greeted every customer who came into the restaurant.

One would be there to shake hands and chat briefly with each customer before customers were seated, or escorted to a waiting area. They displayed broad smiles and a genuine congenial attitude.

While one was greeting customers, the other was working the room – walking from table to table, continuing to chat and make sure their customers were receiving satisfactory service and generally enjoying their meal.

And usually one would make a final check with each customer as they were leaving.

Is it any wonder that restaurant was quite busy, with the waiting area getting plenty of use?

Donna Andersen, an educator who gives instruction on Personal-Touch Teaching to teachers, observed there are no smiles at ATMs.

She cites personal-touch approaches that will result in students becoming more involved in the learning process. An essential, she said, is to listen – really listen.

She said that requires listening with your mouth, with brief comments; listening with your eyes, with your body, and with your heart.

Other skills involved in personal attention – such as remembering names, body language and sensitivity – are noted in Chapter 4 on Personal Relations. Readers may wish to revisit that chapter.

Telephone Etiquette

Too many people simply don't answer their phones. They let voicemail answer instead. But it's not unusual to visit an office and see an employee chatting with a co-worker, playing a computer game or checking personal messages while ignoring a phone ringing on his or her desk.

Yes, phone calls can be interruptions when working. But if it's a problem, managers know problems can grow worse, creating additional problems and expense, if not handled after the initial call or report.

If you don't have time to talk to a caller, say so. Explain your situation and either get a number to return the call, or let the caller know the best time to call back.

Some offices have receptionists who answer the phone with the question "Who's calling?" That is ill-mannered – indicating the answer to whether he or she is available depends on who is calling. And it could be someone returning a call.

But that's still better than getting a recorded response directing you to someone's voice-mail and being forced to leave two or three messages before getting a return call.

We know how much poor telephone etiquette disturbs us; so why treat others that way?

Telephone Time-Savers

Plan in advance for important calls.

Write what you want to cover during a conversation.

Ask if the person you are calling has time to devote to the issue.

Let others know the best times to call you.

Be available when you ask others to call back.

Don't allow others to interrupt your conversation.

7 - Need for Humor

I believe it is <u>impossible</u> to give too much emphasis to the importance of humor in our lives.

Og Mandino, in his book **The Greatest Salesman in the World**, states: "No living creature can laugh except man."

Mandino says: "Trees may bleed when they are wounded, and beasts in the field will cry in pain and hunger.... But only man has the gift of laughter, and it is his to use as he chooses."

Whether animal lovers or experts agree or disagree is not important to this book. What is important, however, is Mandino's next statement.

"I will laugh and my life will be lengthened for this is the great secret of long life ..."

I definitely agree with that!

Unfortunately, many sources used for this book have failed to emphasize that same point.

Even Dale Carnegie, in the voluminous number of good tips and guidelines that he provides, fails in this category. And the same is true in the excellent self-improvement booklets offered by the Jaycees.

Each of those booklets, titled **Communications Dynamics, Personal Dynamics** and **Leadership Dynamics**, has four chapters. And each could use a fifth chapter on humor – even if that fifth chapter is identical in each of those booklets.

As a single man who obtained a divorce in 1995, on various occasions I have turned to the Internet dating services to find friends and meaningful relationships. Nearly all who use those services cite a demand for a sense of humor.

It is humor that breaks tension between individuals.
It is humor that maintains interest in a subject.
It is humor that puts sparkle in a speech.

So now we come to the problem of how!

How do we become humorous? How do we develop humor in ourselves – our speech and our writing?

Writers might try, but books and essays just can't tell us how to be humorous.

Books can provide us with thousands of examples – even hundreds of thousands. But humor is something we must develop on our own. It comes as part of our attitudes and outlook on life.

One of the best items of advice on developing humor comes from the book titled **The Public Speaker's Treasure Chest** by Herbert V. Prochnow and Herbert V. Prochnow Jr.

That book advises that many pertinent stories can be found throughout literature; and the Prochnows strongly recommend reading biographies.

Their book says: "Interesting facts and interesting incidents from interesting lives" can make the difference between the dull or worthwhile and colorful speech or essay. "Searching until one finds this material pays rich rewards."

So again I emphasize <u>READ</u> – the most powerful 4-letter word in our language.

Authors who cite the need to include humor in presentations usually will issue a strong warning that the <u>humor must be related to the topic</u> of the speech or essay.

A touch of humor that brings only a smile, but is inherent to the topic, will outshine any loud guffaws that result from something unrelated to the topic.

Obviously smooth transitions are impossible when the humor is unrelated.

A desire for loud laughter is a common mistake made by many.

Often, the best humor – in writing or speech – is the recounting of an incident or situation that actually happened in the life of the writer or speaker. It comes more naturally – especially in speaking – because it is not something that must be memorized.

Delivery, however, is most important. And delivery usually is a bit easier when the humorous incident comes from our own experiences.

In that respect, the writer has the advantage of revising and rewriting. The speaker, however, must practice delivery to get the best results. Laughs usually depend more on the telling than the plot of a story.

But avoid using puns.

Richard C. Borden, in his book **Public Speaking as Listeners Like It**, advises that a pun rarely gets the laugh that is expected. He says the pun carries with it "an unpleasant connotation of wise-cracking" that listeners dislike.

He says listeners prefer humor in story form.

Humor and various stories to accentuate your writing and speech are available from many sources.

The Prochnows' book is one of two that I bought for that purpose. The other is: **5000 One and Two Liners for Any and Every Occasion,** by Leopold Fechtner.

But, as indicated above, the very best humor usually comes from incidents in our own lives.

Listeners and readers particularly enjoy our humor when we are willing to laugh at ourselves. Many of us tend to be guilty of taking ourselves too seriously. So reporting those incidents when we goofed usually will bring the smiles and chuckles that we desire.

For more than 11 years, I worked with a gal who provided me with a great deal of laughter and daily smiles. Her name is Phyllis Phillips. For many years, she wrote most of the obituaries that appeared in *The Daily Herald* at Provo, Utah.

And the ability to write obituaries almost every day, week after week, definitely requires a sense of humor.

If we had to interrupt her during that duty, her frequent comment was, "Don't bother me; I'm obitching."

And when office bantering occasionally was directed her way, one of her standard comebacks was, "Bite the wall."

It was Phyllis who provided us with ***"The Happy Birthday Dirge,"*** which we started singing when birthdays of newsroom staff members were announced.

And then it became a dubious "honor" for the employees in other departments – when two or three of us were beckoned from the news staff to sing the dirge on their birthdays.

The event brought smiles and chuckles to all involved.

Here are the lyrics of its two stanzas, which <u>must be sung with a quavering voice</u>:

> *Oh Happy Birthday; Oh Happy Birthday.*
> *People dying everywhere;*
> *Gloom and misery in the air;*
> *But Happy Birthday; Oh Happy Birthday.*
> *One step closer to the grave;*
> *Think of all the food we'll save;*
> *But Happy Birthday; Oh Happy Birthday.*

(Phyllis noted her one daughter discovered that dirge, but had no idea of its author.)

67

I left that newspaper in 1983 to become a managing editor in Georgia. But a group of us will never forget the laughter and fun we shared as a result of the dirge.

That fun has continued as I have shared the dirge with many others where I have lived and worked since then – often singing it to someone on his or her birthday.

When in Georgia I met Mike Owen, then a sports editor who was burned out on writing sports. So I assigned him to the news editor's position, but asked him to continue writing a weekly column on any subject of his choosing.

Mike applied a good sense of humor to his writing – similar in style to his favorite humorist, Lewis Grizzard.

I told Mike one day that I was leaving the office shortly for a speaking engagement. I noted I would be explaining newspaper operations at a meeting of retired civil service employees.

When I added that I would probably only be gone for about 45 minutes to an hour, he disputed that statement.

"I expect you'll be gone much longer than that," he said, pointing out that he knew I would be speaking to a large group.

"No, Mike, I'm not a long speaker," I said. I added that I usually only speak for about five to 10 minutes, and then ask for any questions from the audience.

"Oh, you'll be gone longer than that – you'll see," he argued.

When I returned in less than an hour, he remarked:

"I am surprised. I would have bet you would be gone longer."

"I told you so," I said, walking over next to him as he was working at his computer.

"I did just what I told you I would. I talked for no more than 10 minutes and then asked for questions."

And then I decided to tell a little joke on myself, as I leaned over Mike and added: "But I told them everything I know."

Mike got a smirk on his face, as he looked up from his computer and said in a slow, quiet voice:

"You must have told them twice!"

Errors Are Expected

Humor was continually present as a result of working at newspapers. It was something that was needed – because so many stories are serious, disastrous, and depressing.

We also had many bloopers and blunders that appeared in print. Much as we tried to eliminate them, we still expected them – and laughed at them.

Bad headlines, of course, were the most glaring. And they can be found occasionally in almost every newspaper.

Daily newspapers publish as many words as an average book. And they do it in 24 to 48 hours.

On a Sunday, it might be as many words as a thick, hardbound book. On a Monday or Saturday, it might be as few as a small paperback.

That compares with the months that publishers take to produce a book with a similar amount of words. And readers can still find a few errors in those books.

Considering the work volume and limited time, daily newspaper workers expect some errors to slip into print – despite all efforts to eliminate them.

I included that explanation whenever I was asked to speak about my work as a newspaper editor.

We can only wonder how some of those bloopers occurred.

Editors like me were frequently heard muttering something like:

"On what spaceship were we in when we allowed that one to slip through?"

Here are a few examples of headline bloopers – and subsequent comments – that came to my attention recently as I was preparing this chapter:

Kids make nutritious snacks
– Do they taste like chicken?

NEW STUDY OF OBESITY
SEEKS LARGER TEST GROUP
– Weren't they fat enough?

Astronaut takes blame
For gas in spacecraft
– That's what he gets for eating beans!

PANDA MATING FAILS;
VETERINARIAN TAKES OVER
– What a guy! What a guy!

Statistics show that
teen pregnancy drops off
significantly after age 25
– Gee; I wonder why?

I also received some copies of signs that went awry of their purpose. Here are a few of them:

Toilet out of order.
Please use floor below.

Outside a second-hand shop:
We exchange anything – bicycles, washing machines, etc.
Why not bring your wife along and get a wonderful bargain?

Spotted in a safari park:
ELEPHANTS PLEASE STAY IN YOUR CAR

Notice in a farmer's field:
The farmer allows walkers to cross the field for free.
But the bull charges.

Posted at a conference:
For anyone who has children and doesn't know it,
there is a day care on the 1ˢᵗ floor.

Another sign that had me chuckling was one I saw in front of a church when traveling through western Canada. It said:

"Sign broken. Come inside for message."

Common Sense

Common sense must be applied in choices of humor. Avoid items that might be in poor taste. Make your selections suitable for your audience – your listeners, or the readers you are targeting.

On that issue, a simple rule is: If in doubt, don't use it!

Finally, I must repeat an earlier admonition: Don't demand of yourself to find that bit of humor that evokes loud and long laughter. If it's too loud or too long, it can be a distraction from your speech or essay.

Seek instead to draw a couple chuckles and plant smiles on the faces of those in your audience or readership.

What follows are a few samples of my humor writing. They are the short items that I enjoy writing – the type that appear in my first book. I refer to it as soft humor – understatements – designed to have you visualize the incidents in your mind.

Note that each one resulted from incidents in my life, which Borden and the Prochnows consider the best humor to use in a speech. But they also strongly warned that any humor story used must relate to the topic of the speech or essay.

Rusty, the Buick and the Trash Can

Rusty was a gentle soul – a neighborhood gad-about.

He was a big dog of questionable lineage – standing waste-high next to most adults. He was named appropriately as a result of the color of his fur coat.

Rusty would come up to you, wag his tail, visit for a bit to allow you to pat his head and rub his neck. Then he would wonder off, apparently disappointed because you had no snack to offer him.

How muscular and solid Rusty was became evident when he tangled with the Buick in the middle of the street near the end of our block. I guess he just didn't see the Buick when he trotted out in front of it.

I was either in 6th or 7th grade at the time. It was the early 1950s. And back then Buicks were heavy, well-built cars – perhaps the closest that a passenger car ever came to an army tank.

So when Rusty was hit by the Buick and knocked down in the middle of the street, you would expect that he was badly hurt. Only Rusty just got up, shook his head a bit, and trotted off.

But the steel, chrome-plated grille at the front of the Buick did not fare so well. It was caved in.

Now, nearly 60 years later, I can't truthfully tell whether I actually saw the incident, or simply visualized it so vividly when reported to me. And I can still visualize it.

Rusty was the pet of the Stough family who lived in the next block to the west of us. That family had at least three boys and a girl, all of whom were several years older than me. But seldom would you see Rusty with any of them.

So Rusty's gad-about habits were what brought him to the attention of our Dad. I didn't remember the trash can story until my brother, Ron, reminded me of it.

Rusty developed a habit of raiding our trash can, sitting out near the front corner of our garage. And he was smart enough to make his visits the day before trash collection, when he methodically sifted through the can's contents for any tasty delectables, and scattered the rest of its contents.

That disturbed our Dad a bit. He chased Rusty away a few times, but Rusty was adamant about enjoying any goodies that might be available, and soon returned.

He returned just one time too many, prompting our Dad's decision to "fix his wagon." So the trash can lid was wired to provide an electrical charge the next time Rusty was spotted approaching it.

Our Dad's impatience with the problem was rewarded.

Rusty's shock resulted in some mournful howls as he

gingerly trotted off through the neighboring   yards, shaking one paw after another.

Although that ended the problem, our Dad apparently felt guilty as he told Mr. Stough about the incident. Mr. Stough was disturbed only by the fact that he was not there to witness the event.

# # #

Dating – Pennsylvania Dutch Style

My father – Lester Berkheimer – was a man of many stories.

It was a characteristic prevalent throughout his family, including his five brothers and three sisters. And it was part of the Pennsylvania Dutch society in which they were reared.

Pennsylvania Dutch is considered a low German dialect that all of his family could understand and speak. I only wish I had learned it.

That Pennsylvania Dutch society spawned many stories such as the one about farm "boy" John Kunkle, told by my Dad. In those days, courting – dating – was done by horse and buggy. I don't know if the story really happened; but it's certainly worth telling.

The day after John turned 21 years old, he was greeted with this comment from his father:

"Vell, son, your ma and I talked it over last night, and ve think it's time you be thinkin' of marryin'."

Now John, a husky farm boy, never acted as if he gave much thought to courtin' and marriage. He was dressed that morning in his everyday stomper boots and work coveralls, with binder-twine in place of one torn shoulder strap.

Caught off guard, and stammering a bit, John said:

"I ... I ain't paid much attention to the girls of marryin' age. Who could I see?"

Having already discussed that with his ma, his pa replied:

"You could start with Jakie March down the road. You know he has three. There's the tellyphone. Go ring him up."

After cranking the operator on the old wall-mounted phone, and asking for the March house, John asked:

"Is that you, Jakie March? I'm John Kunkle up the road."

"Ya; this is Jakie. Vhat can I do fer ya, John?"

"Vell, since yestiddy, I'm 21, and pa and ma say I should be thinkin' of marryin'. You have some girls, don't ya?"

"Ya. Ve got three. Sarah's the oldest, and the one you should be thinkin' about. She can carry two full buckets of water."

Then John reported he didn't know if he could make it over today, because he was just about to hitch up the team and head for some work in the fields.

"But; now vait a minute," John said. "I'll be spreadin' manure in the field across the lane from your house this afternoon. Tell Sarah I'll be there about ..."

Can you imagine that? Dating by manure spreader!

# # #

Hakie and the Chimney

One of my Pennsylvania Dutch uncles, who grew up at a time when many people were known by their nicknames, tells a good story about the building of a chimney.

My uncle was known by everyone as "Pud." How he got that name is another story, but I'm sure many folks did not even know his given name. And I may have been a high school senior before I learned that it was George.

Uncle Pud enjoyed telling the story about Hakie, the chimney, and the doctor who had a reputation for taking months to pay his bills. I believe I heard it at least twice. But I was amazed when one of his daughters told me recently that she never heard it.

The doctor was adding a recreation room to his house, and Hakie agreed to build the fireplace and chimney. Uncle Pud was a contractor and Hakie often did work for my uncle. So Uncle Pud warned Hakie about the doctor's reputation.

Perhaps a week after the project was completed, the doc called Hakie to complain that the chimney didn't draw properly. He said he started to make a fire in the fireplace and smoke began filling his new recreation room.

Hakie told the doc that if he was ready to pay for the project the next day, Hakie would stop by to make sure his chimney would work properly.

So the next day, after the doc paid him, Hakie got a ladder off his truck and leaned it against the doc's house. Then he went back to his truck, got several small rocks and took them with him as he went up the ladder onto the doc's roof.

Hakie climbed over to the chimney where he threw the rocks down into the chimney. Then he came back down the ladder and told the doc: "Now your chimney will work."

Uncle Pud explained that Hakie had cemented a window pane across the inside of the chimney about 5 or 6 layers of brick down from the top!

# # #

Tales of our absent-minded actions and the in-house bantering that occurs in offices and between family members are other good sources of humor.

I recall when the company that processes debit cards for my bank committed a major blunder, which affected me and several other customers, including one of the bank's employees.

The company failed to mail out new debit cards before the old ones expired.

It was rather embarrassing that Saturday when a clerk reported payment was denied because my debit card had expired.

On Monday an express delivery to my bank was arranged for the new card. The bank called me when it arrived on Wednesday.

So for several days I knew that my old card was useless.

But on the drive to the bank to get my new card, I tried to buy gas with the old card!

Duh!

And I remember one day when I was news editor at a daily newspaper. I was advised at noon-time to tell the staff the computer system was off line and would not be available for a couple hours because of maintenance programming.

"Okay, I'll warn the staff," I replied. So I went to my desk, sat down and started to write a note in the computer telling the staff the computer was down.

Then I looked around sheepishly to see if anyone realized what I was trying to do!

Patrick F. McManus, a northern Idaho outdoor writer, is one of my favorite humorists. His short stories are interesting and easy to read – except for his frequent long paragraphs when he's not writing dialogue.

Many are about incidents in his youth – similar to the type of stories told by Bill Cosby and Garrison Keillor

His many humor columns, which appeared in outdoor magazines, were turned into at least a dozen books.

# # #

Forms of Humor

Adviser: The comic adviser gives uncalled for advice in a "punch" prototype. Example: Advice to people who want to buy a puppy. Don't.

Anecdotes: Any interesting event – either having to do with a celebrity, or something smaller, that helps the humorist make a point. Anecdotes are great for both writers and speakers.

Aside: A thought added as if something the speaker was saying reminded him of it.

Banter: Good-natured teasing back and forth; an exchange of witty remarks.

Blendword: Blending two or three words to make a new word. Example: smog for smoke and fog.

Blue Humor: Not appropriate for the public speaker. Humor based on easily offensive subjects like making love, body parts, and bodily functions.

Blunder (or blooper): Wit based on a mistake, which makes the person or the situation appear foolish.

Bull: A humorous statement that is based on an outrageous contradiction.
Example: The best people have never had kids.

Burlesque: A form of satire. Burlesque ridicules any basic style of speech or writing. (Parody makes fun of specific writings.)

Caricature: Exaggeration of a person's mental, physical, or personality traits – in wisecrack form.

The Catch Tale: A funny story that messes up the reader or listener by implying an awful ending but then stopping with a small declaration.

Conundrum: A word puzzle that can't be solved because the answer is a pun.
Example: Why do cows wear bells? Their horns don't work.

Epigram: A clever, short saying about a general group. Mostly satire about mankind. There are two types: wordplay and thought play.

Exaggerism: An exaggerated witticism that overstates a feature, defect, or strangeness of someone or something.

Freudian Slip: A funny statement that seems to just pop out, but which actually comes from subconscious thoughts.

Hyperbole: Extreme exaggeration.

Irony: A leading part of humor. Irony is using words to express something completely different from literal meaning. Usually, someone says the opposite of what they mean and the listener believes the opposite of what they said.

Joke: A short story ending with a funny, climactic twist.

Nonsensism: This type includes the epigram and the wisecrack. It is any kind of funny nonsense in speaking form. Nonsensism includes all kinds of absurdity without logic, making a generally absurd observation.

Parody: A humorous version of any well-known writing.

Practical Joke: A joke put into action. You hear an oral joke, see a printed joke, but feel the practical joke. The trick is played on another person and the humor comes from what happens.

Pun: A classic play on words that sound similar but have different meanings.
　　Example: What do you have if 20 rabbits in a row all back up one step? A receding hare line.

Recovery: A combination of blunder and wit, where a person makes an error, and then makes a fast correction.

Repartee: Includes clever replies and retorts. The most common form is the insult.

Satire: Wit that is critical humor. Satire is sarcasm that makes fun of something.

Situational Humor: This is comedy that comes from your own life. No one in your audience will have heard it and it can get a group used to you. This type of humor is based on a humorous situation that you have experienced.

Switching: A common form of switching is changing the main parts of the story – such as the setup or the punch line – and creating a new joke.

Understatement: Making something that is regular or large seem extremely smaller or less. Intentionally downsizing a major situation or large object. It might be considered the opposite of Exaggerism.

Wisecrack: Any clever remark about a particular person or thing. Wisecracks usually are quick wordplays about a person.

Wit: Humor, irony, sarcasm, satire, repartee. Wit is funny because of the sudden sharpness and quick perception. Wit can bite. Verbal wit is a type of humor known as wordplay.

8 - Persuasion

You can make a difference in our world when you can persuade and influence others.

We all have that opportunity.

When we learn to influence and persuade others, we also are learning the tasks of marketing and sales.

All of us participate in the selling process throughout our lives. Even if we are not engaged in marketing products and services, we are involved in selling our ideas and ourselves.

In doing so, there is one very important concept that we must impress permanently in our minds. It is this statement:

Other people do things for their reasons, ...

not because I want them to.

That is perhaps the most important concept explained in Dale Carnegie's book –

How to Win Friends and Influence People.

In returning to his book, we also return to that <u>most powerful 4-letter word in the English language – READ.</u>

During my 28-year newspaper career, I wrote many columns and editorials that were designed to sway opinion, stir action and laud the good examples set by others.

The greatest rewards were the praising comments I received from many readers.

In addition, my newspaper editorials won awards in both Utah and Texas.

Much of that was a result of reading Carnegie's book. And many times I repeated his advice on why others do what they do.

When we keep in mind the concept that other folks do things for their reasons, not ours – we can persuade, influence and sell.

To act on that concept, we must discover the reasons that prompt others to act, and then emphasize those issues in what we are saying or writing.

For instance, a car salesman must quickly learn what color is preferred, and whether power or economy with safety is wanted.

And again, we must emphasize the importance of the beginning.

In speaking – whether to one person or several – always smile and present a friendly appearance.

In writing, your words must establish a friendly tone.

Dale Carnegie says: **"When you wish to win people to your way of thinking, begin in a friendly way."**

That is the first of my 10 rules for persuading others through speaking and writing.

Carnegie lists 12 rules that apply to one-on-one situations for influencing and selling ideas to others. But they are directed to speaking only.

I reshuffled his concepts into a somewhat different list – so they apply to writing as well as speaking.

1 -- Begin in a friendly way.

In speaking, a smile is required when you begin. And in both speaking and writing, it's best to begin by praising something well done – or simply make a pleasing observation – before turning to the issue.

2 -- Respect the Views of Others.

In speaking, this requires you to follow that first of Carnegie's rules. He states the only way to get the best of an argument or disagreement is to avoid it.

He observes that even when you win an argument, by shooting the other person's views full of holes, you still lose. You lose because you have done 3 things:

- **You made the other person feel inferior;**
- **You hurt that person's pride, and**
- **You created resentment toward you.**

Carnegie adds: "A man convinced against his will

Is of the same opinion still."

When we show respect for the views of others, we will refrain from writing or saying other views "are wrong."

In speaking, it is imperative to honestly try to see things through the views of others. And Carnegie advises that not only must we try to understand their views, but we must be sympathetic to their ideas and desires.

In writing, we must acknowledge that some readers will have different views. So we must avoid criticizing opposing views and concentrate on simply citing the reasons for choosing our positions.

3 -- Give Facts, Cite Sources and Dramatize Ideas.

Be sure that what you present as facts actually are facts – and not simply opinions or conclusions.

Studies and research often provide conclusions that might remain open to different interpretations and be subject to further research. So be sure to emphasize those sources.

Historical statistics, however, usually are facts that remain irrefutable.

You can sway readers and listeners more easily when you dramatize your ideas and concepts with examples. Cite situations that readers and listeners can identify with – such as the many similar experiences we all had when we were young.

4 -- Be Quick to Admit a Mistake ...

or That You Might Be Wrong.

We seldom get into trouble in our relationships with others if we are willing to admit that we might be wrong.

That usually will end all argument and inspire an opponent to be as fair and open-minded as we are.

And if we definitely are wrong, we must admit it immediately and emphatically.

We must do so in writing as well as speaking if the original mistake or error occurred in writing.

Isn't it easier to say you goofed than to suffer vehement condemnation from others after trying to gloss over or hide your mistake?

Don't we wish politicians would think that way?

My newspaper columns were called "Berky's Babblings." I selected that name purposely to avoid upsetting readers who strongly disagreed. I reasoned that then they could say: "Oh well; he's just babbling."

5 -- Let Others Do the Telling and Asking.

When attempting to sell a product or service, let customers do most of the talking. Let others tell you their needs and desires. It is your job to be of service by attempting to meet those desires.

Similarly, if you are tackling an issue in speech or writing, you must show how the desires of your readers or audience can be realized.

When attempting to convince a group to "buy" your concept, service or idea, it is wise to shift quickly from telling what you have to offer to providing answers to questions.

In writing, <u>we must anticipate the questions of readers</u> and provide the appropriate information.

6 -- Use Wording that Draws Yes, Yes Responses.

Ask questions and use statements that you know will draw agreement.

The more areas of agreement that you can establish, the better your chances of reaping the desired result.

7 -- Write and Talk in Terms
of Advantages and Disadvantages.

This is how we avoid making the mistake of saying what is wrong or right. In addition, it might be advisable to refrain from saying what to do or not to do.

In writing, it usually is advisable to limit your effort to improving or changing only one issue or idea.

8 -- Let Others Determine the Idea Was Theirs.

One of our former presidents – I believe it was Ronald Reagan – had a sign on his desk that said: There is no limit to what you can accomplish when you are willing to allow others to take the credit.

In both writing and speaking. It is wise to use phraseology that establishes the basis for others to draw their own conclusion – a conclusion that we planned to establish with a logical presentation.

9 -- Appeal to Noble Motives.

Often, you will reap the appropriate action by appealing to a pride in honesty and fair play in the audience.

10 -- Sometimes It's Best to Issue a Challenge.

A challenge can initiate a sense of competition that spawns a desire for improvement or change.

And challenges can be fun. I have been involved with several organizations when various challenges were issued – in attempts to sell more tickets, increase fundraising or recruit new members.

I had to take a banana cream pie in the face when I lost one such challenge. That's another tale in my *Stories from The Golden Throne.*

One final note: As emphasized earlier in this book, strive for brevity and simplicity in all presentations.

Some Examples

At the beginning of this chapter, I noted that we all have the opportunity to promote change and influence others through persuasion.

Some of us – such as salesmen – will strive to persuade through normal conversation.

Others may be more capable of influencing people through speeches and debating events.

And then there are those – like myself – who prefer attempting to influence others through writing.

Some who use writing are engaged in drafting advertisements. Others write editorials and interpretive articles for various media.

As a retiree, I've turned to letters to the editor, essays and books.

What follows are two of my letters to the editor and a couple editorials. They display various examples of my 10 rules. All of them were previously published.

Finally, this chapter will end with my Tips for Debating, also published previously.

Dangers at Interstate Ramps

(Published as a Letter to the Editor)

The road crews in Montana and its counties deserve praise for the good work they do in snow removal each year along the state's major highways. But one failure presents a danger that could result in serious injuries and one or more deaths.

I believe Montana has a nationwide reputation for doing a good job in snow removal – especially when people consider how often it snows in Montana.

When I was driving a tractor-trailer rig coast-to-coast, I never worried about traveling over Montana's passes. For example, Montana always had its portion of Lookout Pass well sanded.

But for the past several years, I noticed that Montana often fails to carry that good work over to the exit and entrance ramps.

With the interstate highways relatively clear – especially in the right lanes – many drivers in Montana will continue to travel at or near the 65 and 75 mph speed limits. But if they fail to slow down more than usual when approaching an exit ramp, they could be in serious trouble.

Another danger exists at the entrance ramps, which are designed for drivers to accelerate their vehicles so they can safely merge at interstate speeds when they reach the end of the ramp. That can be quite impossible when the entrance ramp has not been cleared of ice and snow.

If deaths occur, or some motorists are maimed as a result of the state's failure to clear the ramps – the state could face some major adverse reactions – perhaps even lawsuits.

For safety's sake – and to eliminate or reduce such potential problems – Montana needs to do a better job at those expressway ramps.

# # #

Notice how that example begins in a friendly way by praising the good overall work before citing an area in need of improvement – the first rule listed above.

It attempts to present a positive view of what is needed and why -- citing potential negative results if positive action is not taken.

It also shows how dramatizing and issue can make it more effective.

I have noticed some improvement at the ramps in the Butte area since that letter was published.

The next example ends with a question designed to have most people agreeing and saying yes.

Motorcycle Helmets Issue

(Published as a Letter to the Editor)

I have noticed that Montana's helmet law for motorcycle riders is applicable only to riders who are 17 and under. That concerns me!

Years ago, I was against motorcycle helmet laws. Back then I considered it was just their tough luck if motorcycle riders turned themselves into a vegetable because they were too macho to wear a helmet.

But that was before I realized that my insurance premiums – and the premiums paid by others – can and do go up when motorcycle riders maim themselves.

Accident statistics affect the actuarial tables used by all insurance companies. Even those accidents by motorcyclists covered by other insurance companies can affect the premiums that we must pay.

That means the hospital and treatment costs paid by any insurance company as a result of motorcycle accidents will affect the rates paid by everybody.

The bottom line is: I do not want to pay more for my insurance because some motorcyclists are too macho to wear helmets.

I believe motorcyclists should be required to pay more for their insurance if they don't want to wear helmets.

So my question to everyone else is: Do you want to pay more because they aren't required to wear helmets?

# # #

This next example was part of a three-editorials entry that won Utah's annual editorials writing contest – open to all media members in the state. The honor included a cash award of $100, which I received.

Why Not Wednesday Deer Open?

Opening weekend of the Utah general deer season has made it clear Utah lawmakers need to do more than require all license holders to take the hunter safety course.

Opening weekend – and most particularly opening day – has become a chaotic circus at best, and a downright disaster to many who had hoped to enjoy a safe and sane outing, let alone take home some meat.

And with each year's opener, less sanity and less safety are apparent.

How can anyone enjoy both a safe, sane deer hunt when hunters are spaced about every 75 to 100 yards?

How can anyone enjoy the camping experience when a hunter must drive to the end of a dead-end road on a ridge more than 9,000 feet high to find a secluded camping area?

Who enjoys camping bumper-to-bumper in RV cities?

Is it any wonder disheartened and discouraged hunters turn to road-hunting by the opening-day afternoon when the morning's insanity brings hunter orange too close for comfort from every direction?

One hunter, for example, reported it was "too dangerous" after bullets whined near him on opening day, sending him home that evening.

Some Uinta National Forest rangers call it "opening day mania," and add even they won't go hunting on the opening weekend.

A couple of foresters remarked that it's gone so far, hunters can't even find a parking space along the main roads of the Uinta National Forest.

But what one forest supervisor finds so sad is that apparently almost no one cares – and that no one is trying to do anything about the situation.

So it's time for some of us to do something!

Big game management involves more than just promoting the greatest number of game animals for the available habitat. It also should involve managing hunting pressure.

Some ideas and possible alternatives:

- The big game board could schedule a mid-week opener for the deer hunt – such as the one for the elk season, which opens on a Wednesday. Maybe that would reduce the opening-day mania.

- Limit deer licenses to every other year for each hunter.

State Division of Wildlife Resources workers won't like selling only half as many licenses each year unless they can charge twice as much. But anyone who is disgusted with the opening crowds should be agreeable to that.

- Try splitting the deer season – like a couple other western states have done.

Colorado and New Mexico did so, and forest workers noted pressure was reduced substantially on forest roads and facilities.

- The foresters here have made the following suggestion: Have a three-day opener; then close the hunt for three days. Open again for a second season of five days; then close for another three days. Then open for a final season of seven days.

With that arrangement, hunters would be allowed to seek a permit for only one of the three seasons.

These suggestions are not the only options available, but it's evident something should be done to reduce pressure and return safety to the deer hunt.

# # #

This example establishes somewhat of a challenge to lawmakers and wildlife managers. And it appeals to noble motives.

It cites sources, dramatizes ideas and strives to have readers agree with the statements and ideas.

The next example dramatizes an issue with questions after breaking one of the rules above.

Drinking ruling was a mistake

(Originally published in *The Big Spring Herald*, Texas)

We believe the Texas Supreme Court made a mistake this fall when it ruled that bar owners can be held legally liable in traffic deaths caused by drunken drivers who earlier had been patrons at the bar.

What a ludicrous decision.

We can only hope that the Supreme Court justices were half asleep, distracted or otherwise had an off day when they issued that ruling.

Whatever happened to that universal principle of accepting responsibility for our own actions – the one our parents strived so hard to teach us?

It makes us think of when we were back in elementary school – when we tried to name others to blame for our actions. You remember – when you told your teacher, your mother or dad, that John Henry made you do it.

Let's examine this situation in more detail.

The ruling says if someone walks into a tavern, gets drunk and kills somebody else, we can blame the tavern owners.

Is the next step to hold beer distributors and liquor stores responsible for drunken drivers and destructive party-goers?

Will organizations, or even homeowners, be held liable because someone attended their party, got drunk, then went out and killed someone else?

What about someone who went to four or five taverns and had a couple drinks at each? Should only the last one be sued? The last two ... or maybe all of them?

Put yourself in the place of the bartenders in a busy tavern. How is that bartender to know who is driving and who are passengers? With a half-dozen people wanting drinks at the same time, should the bartender be expected to survey each before serving them?

We acknowledge that alcoholism and drunken driving are serious problems – and that sensible steps should be taken to reduce or eliminate abuses. But let's put the blame where it belongs – on the person consuming those drinks, not the one who's serving them.

Let's not allow money-grubbing attorneys to haul whomever they can into court just because the drunken driver or his estate has little or no money.

The Texas Supreme Court should admit it made a mistake and correct it as quickly as possible.

# # #

That example fails to follow the second rule advising "to avoid" criticizing the views of others. And it deliberately does so for effect – to dramatize how terrible the ruling was in the considered opinion of the newspaper.

It also emphasizes that the ruling is counter to the values that many of us were taught in school and by our parents. Sometimes there is no escaping the need to say that something is just plain wrong.

# # #

Tips for Debating

(The following article on debating was provided as a guide to students attending the course on Improving Communications.)

A few years ago, I had the privilege of serving as a judge at a regional high school speech competition.

Hundreds of students participated in the competition, and many local residents volunteered to serve as judges.

I felt qualified to be a judge after years of writing editorials, speaking to readers about newspaper subjects, and my activities as a member and president of a Toastmasters chapter.

I thought the students in the Extemporaneous competition did rather well considering the little time they had to prepare their talk.

In contrast, I concluded that the students in the debate competition that I judged needed considerably more instruction and coaching – in both how to prepare and present their positions.

The debate contest began with one student reading a proposal.

She read entirely too fast and with little voice inflection. I could not understand what she was saying.

I stopped her – not just once, but three times. Each time I emphasized: "You will have to go slower and pronounce your words succinctly if you expect me to understand what you are saying."

She ignored me.

She droned on for perhaps 3 to 5 minutes. I did not understand what she was proposing until near the end.

That is not how you win a debate. Nor is it how you will sway opinions in real life.

Is it any wonder why she and her teammate lost in that debate?

I drove home that day telling myself that the students needed considerably more instruction and coaching in how to organize and present a winning argument.

And I decided that I should be able to write an outline on how best to present winning oral arguments. After all, it's not much different than writing editorials – something I did for many years.

The one major difference is: The opposition also will have opportunities to speak. That merely places more emphasis on research and knowing the subject well – the first steps in preparation.

So let's keep it simple and divide the debate instruction into two phases – **Preparation** and **Presentation**. The two are equally important.

You might be excellent at presenting your position – but lose to an opposition that was better prepared.

Nor does it matter how well you have prepared, if your presentation fails to persuade your audience – be they judges, other listeners or readers.

The **Preparation** includes:
  Research

- *Listing advantages and disadvantages*
- *Preparing one or two note cards on the top 3 to 5 advantages*
- *Identifying the top 3 to 5 disadvantages*
- *Preparing one or two note cards on rebuttals to the top disadvantages*
- *Listing lesser disadvantages and being prepared to negate them by returning to the top advantages*

The **Presentation** must include:
- *Simple declarative sentences*
- *Conviction*
- *Salesmanship – persuasion*
- *Rebuttals*
- *Practice*

Let's be specific about each of those items.

There's no need to waste time on explaining **research**. You can't win debates or persuade individuals if you haven't done research to thoroughly know the subject.

Listing advantages and disadvantages of your proposal also are self-explanatory. Obviously you can't prepare appropriate rebuttals if you are not familiar with the potential disadvantages.

Now comes the important meat of your argument. Decide on the top 3 to 5 advantages of your position – be it affirmative or negative – and know those points extremely well.

List those top 3 to 5 points with a few key words about each on only one or two 3x5 note cards – no more than two cards and preferable only one.

If you can't do that, then you don't know the subject well enough to speak convincingly about it. Also, the fewer notes you have to look at, the more you will look at your audience.

Eye contact is extremely important.

Next, **identify and study the top disadvantages**. And prepare another one or two note cards with the key points of rebuttal to those disadvantages.

Then, if your opposition refers to lesser disadvantages, be prepared to point out how your major advantages simply overwhelm those lesser issues.

In presentation, the best effects come from **simple, to-the-point sentences**. And you can get even more effect by pausing occasionally and slowly repeating a major point to allow it to sink into your audience.

Notice how I sometimes separate phrases with dashes before and after. Those dashes signify a slightly longer pause than commas, and give a bit more effect to those phrases.

And you must be able to speak with conviction – showing that you believe in what you are saying. This may take a bit of acting – but only a slight bit. Over-acting will quickly be spotted and can work against you.

But ask yourself: How can I be convincing if I can't display that I'm convinced?

You also must be a **salesman** – because you are selling an idea.

Dale Carnegie, in his book entitled "How to Win Friends and Influence People," emphasized one basic point: People do things for their reasons – not yours or mine.

To sway the folks in your audience, then, you must try to put yourself in their positions and determine what issues and arguments will matter most to them.

In your **rebuttal**, you must minimize the effects of the disadvantages cited by your opposition, and then return – again and again – to those points and issues that you think will have the most effect on your audience.

Do not allow yourself to be drawn into wasting precious persuasion time on lesser details with minimum effect. You must be fully aware of them, and then be prepared to simply state – bluntly – that their effect will be minimal and "will pale in significance" to the advantages that you have cited.

Practice also is self-explanatory. Practice stating your position to your boyfriend, girlfriend, mother, father, brother, sister, spouse or whoever will listen and offer any criticisms.

If you can't give a convincing argument to those who want to believe you, how can you do so to those who may **not** want to believe you?

Finally, a good debater should not be reading anything.

The only rare exception might be a short passage of a couple sentences that someone else wrote – but only if it adds an especially effective emphasis to a particular point that a debater wants to make.

Reading anything else is an indication to the audience that the speaker does not know the subject well.

# # #

9 – Role of Leadership

(And Management)

I have often heard the same complaint!

It makes me wonder why so many companies don't do a better job of training their supervisors.

I heard the complaint again while wondering how to begin this chapter – when a repairman came into my home.

I mentioned that I was working on a leadership and management article, and he said:

"Don't get me started on management!

"All management wants to do is nitpick on little things. It doesn't seem to matter how hard we try, we don't receive any praise – just complaints."

His comments prompted me to wonder if his management had received appropriate training in leadership.

The proper role of management is leadership. So any discussion on good management should begin with an examination of leadership.

Each of us has served as a leader occasionally during our lives. That occurred whenever we announced our decision to do something, and one or more others decided to join us.

Any discussion of leadership also must return to the emphasis on people skills cited in Chapter 4.

The famous public speaker Cavett Robert once said:

"First, foremost and above all else, we are in the people business. A person prepared 'knowledge - wise' and not conditioned 'people-wise' is just a failure walking around looking for a place to happen."

The Key is Serving

Formal leadership and management should be considered synonymous.

Formal leadership involves making decisions and achieving results through others. To get the best results, however, leaders and managers must serve those who they direct.

That's the key word to proper leadership and management – "serving."

Poorly trained managers have the misconception that employees are hired to simply do as they are told by their supervisors. That's the wrong attitude.

Employees know that they have been hired to serve the company – and that they must take directions from their supervisors.

Supervisors and managers, in turn, are expected to be leaders. And as leaders, they face the dual roles of serving both the company and the employees.

Unfortunately, their role of serving the employees receives too little emphasis.

It is the obligation of leaders and supervisors to serve workers by providing:

▰ The needed training in knowledge and skills;
▰ The necessary tools and supplies;
▰ Written job descriptions that detail duties;
▰ Assistance in personal growth and problem-solving, and
▰ Frequent appraisals on performance.

The first three are simple and easy to understand. But the last two are multi-faceted with a host of issues.

Those issues include respect, attitudes, motivation, employee goals and personal problems.

The best motivational approach is the fostering of good attitudes toward the supervisor and company. That requires treating workers with respect and fairness.

Although the need for frequent work appraisals is last in the list above, it is perhaps the most important in fostering good attitudes in workers.

How Good Leaders Operate

■ Good leaders will frequently tell a worker – both orally and in written memos – that he or she is appreciated for doing excellent or good work.

A sincere compliment is one of the most effective teaching and motivational methods in existence.

■ Good leaders discuss employee performance deficiencies in private.

It is particularly important, however, to be specific about the area needing improvement, and to note those duties that are being performed well.

In addition, the meeting must be directed toward discussing positive ideas to help the employee improve in the deficient area. A supervisor can't expect positive results from negative actions.

I recall taking a problem to the publisher when I was a local news editor. After outlining the problem and discussing it, the publisher concluded the meeting by advising: "The next time you bring a problem to me, I will expect you to also bring some suggested solutions or options to resolve the issue."

Good leaders must be prepared with positive suggestions.

■ Good leaders will show that they care about workers and their problems.

Supervisors should assist a worker in resolving both work-related and personal problems – because performance is affected.

Helping workers resolve personal problems promotes better attitudes as well as improved performance.

■ Good supervisors will learn the personality and goals of each employee.

Managers should assist workers in progressing toward their goals – as long as those goals are not contradictory to the company's objectives.

■ Good leaders analyze strengths and weaknesses of each worker, and then guide workers to those areas where they are most capable.

In addition, they will assist them in overcoming weaknesses through more training.

■ Good managers will provide enough operational flexibility in job descriptions to allow workers the opportunity to learn new and additional tasks – toward advancing themselves.

■ Good leaders realize there is no limit to what you can accomplish if you don't care who gets the credit.

Also, in discussing how supervisors and managers should operate, you will note that I do not, and will not, use the term "superior."

Just because someone has the title of manager or supervisor, they should never be considered superior to those they direct and assist.

Each of us has talents of one type or another. A person may be superior in one area while others are superior in other areas.

I didn't note the source, but my communications notes included this quotation: "A person who talks about his inferiors hasn't any."

The Effects of Tone

The tone that a manager has in discussions with employees is just as important as what the manager is saying.

I recall when a newspaper where I was working was sold by one syndicate to another group. The new owner sent a couple main office executives to talk to our staff.

One of those executives said:

"In today's economy there are two types of workers. There are those workers who are overworked and underpaid. And there are those workers who are unemployed."

Unfortunately, he made those remarks with a threatening tone. His remarks came across as if he was saying: "So you better shape up; or don't let the door hit you in the butt on your way out."

He could have used his remarks to good advantage if he had softened his tone with one or two positive comments. For instance, he could have suggested that supervisors will be glad to meet with staff members to discuss any concerns about what is expected.

But that threatening attitude also was displayed by the new publisher sent to replace the one fired by the new owner. And that attitude resulted in three department chiefs leaving that newspaper. I was one of them.

The Necessity of Trust

Some years ago, an article in the magazine *Supervisory Management* discussed the need for a company to build a feeling of trust through its communications.

The article noted the two major factors that are behind most corporate problems – lack of training and lack of trust.

The article observed the value of trust in increasing productivity has been known and hailed for decades by communication specialists, psychologists, company presidents and human relations experts.

"Trust is at the core of every relationship!" the article stated as it went on to cite the problems that occur in a non-trusting environment.

In such an environment, people won't tell of their thoughts and concerns. They will:

- *Hoard information;*
- *Fail to report the severity of a problem;*
- *Doubt even the most valid messages from management, and*
- *Waste enormous amounts of energy protecting themselves.*

The results are lower morale, high absenteeism, high turnover, and an undetermined loss in wasted potential.

Trust relates directly to communications credibility.

A company that maintains "transparency" – the latest buzzword for openness – will enhance its credibility, especially with its employees.

It is not necessary to agree with a person's opinion to gain that person's respect.

In fact, it's just the opposite. The more we trust someone, the more comfortable we are in expressing our differences, and the more at ease we are in our communications.

The degree of trust between a worker and supervisor affects both the quality and quantity of their communication and interaction.

Trust begins with top management and can saturate the climate of an organization. Only when top management speaks openly and candidly will people develop trust.

Contrary to what some people believe, self-disclosure – within the bounds of good judgment – does not create the impression of weakness or reduce respect.

Instead, a willingness to share information, and discuss weak areas, indicates self-security and encourages others to do the same, which enhances relationships.

Trust and self-disclosure promote:

- *Timely and accurate information when needed;*
- *Reports about situations before they reach crisis levels;*
- *Disclosure of problems early so that less costly solutions remain feasible;*
- *Commitment to improved policies and decisions;*
- *Honest, supportive relationships;*
- *Maximum credibility, with less unproductive suspicion and hostility, and*
- *More individual creativeness.*

With trust comes power – because real power is earned, not awarded as a result of a title.

From a position of authority, someone can issue autocratic commands. But that person will never get the deeper commitment and response that are available by creating a trusting environment with open communications.

Real power comes from credibility. And credibility comes from a combination of perceived competence, trust and a dynamic ability to turn words into action.

In the face of all this evidence, how can anyone deny that trust is the key factor in determining the quality of a work environment?

The Best Leaders

The best leaders sometimes are not the most brilliant people. But the best leaders will have one significant ability: They will know how to make timely and sound decisions based on good advice.

The best leader may not be an expert in any one field. But that leader will be smart enough to surround himself with experts, and then take advice only from the expert most knowledgeable about the issue involved.

Theodore Roosevelt said:

"The best executive is the one who has sense enough to pick good men to do what he wants done, and self-restraint enough to keep from meddling with them while they do it."

Good managers do not try to micro-manage. When assigning work and projects, they detail the results they expect and allow a reasonable time limit.

And companies with good management and good policies reap the benefits of low employee turnover. High turnover necessitates continual costly training and the problems associated with less stability.

Inflexibility Issues

The best leaders also realize the need for flexibility.

Many of the problems that customer service employees face result from management's failure to provide enough operational flexibility.

Inflexibility creates the "red tape" complaints generated by bureaucracies – whether they be government bureaucracies or company bureaucracies.

Good managers and good companies are familiar with Pareto's Principle – the 80-20 rule. That's when 80 percent of your sales come from 20 percent of your customers; and when 80 percent of your problems come from 20 percent of your patrons, or 20 percent of your employees.

Pareto's Principle also means that policies and procedures established by both companies and government can be expected to cover only 80 percent of the issues – because 20 percent of circumstances simply cannot be foreseen or anticipated.

To deal with that 20 percent, good managers realize the necessity of training front-line employees – those who deal directly with the public – in the art of using discretion and bending or breaking the rules a bit to resolve the situation.

It's the art of "rolling with the punches" – an often used analogy referring to the sport of boxing.

A good example is the flexibility necessary in newspaper publishing.

I recall one day when the afternoon newspaper where I worked was ready to start the press. Deadlines had been met, and I was conducting the final perusal of the front page I had designed when we received word that President Ronald Reagan was shot.

That day staff workers in several departments cooperated to quickly rearrange the paper to add four full pages as I redesigned the front page.

We needed to accommodate both photos and stories resulting from the shooting, plus continuing new developments in a couple other stories.

Not all last-minute events were that drastic, but newspaper managers know that staff flexibility is necessary to deal with an airplane crash, city fire, or any other major event that occurs at deadline time.

The need for some flexibility with procedures was emphasized to me years ago by a sarcastic comment. The comment came from Charlie Zumwalt, the composing room foreman at *The Daily Herald* at Provo, Utah, when I was an editor there.

Charlie said: ***"We can't let progress get in the way of procedures."***

With that comment I realized that sometimes we may need to bend, ignore or change a procedure when that procedure becomes an obstacle to our original objectives.

So good managers come to realize they must provide some degree of flexibility in procedures and policies to accommodate unforeseen circumstances and changing conditions.

Usually that can be accomplished by training employees in how to deal with unexpected situations – to use discretion.

When employees are adequately trained, small problems won't develop into larger, crisis issues. And fewer issues will be taken to customer service workers.

Companies with large customer service staffs likely are failing to provide adequate training to the front line workers who deal daily with the public.

Successful Bosses

An October, 2012, internet article identified the six personality traits common to the most successful bosses.

The Yahoo article, by Geoffrey James, cites a statistical analysis of data on sales managers. It states that "successful bosses tend to be:

- *"Humble rather than arrogant;*
- *"Flexible rather than rigid;*
- *"Straightforward rather than evasive;*
- *"Forward thinking rather than improvisational;*
- *"Precise rather than vague," and*
- *"Patient rather than ill-tempered."*

The article observed that "successful bosses put themselves and their own egos into the background," and focus on "coaching employees to perform to their highest potential."

It added that successful bosses prepare their employees to make the best decisions by providing them with the necessary information – "even if that information is difficult or sensitive."

It said successful bosses thoroughly explained plans and goals "so that there was no ambiguity."

# # #

If managers and supervisors work at using the leadership techniques detailed in this chapter, they will face fewer problems and others will hear fewer complaints such as the one cited by the repairman at the beginning of this chapter.

What follows are copies of guides on personnel management, delegating work, and how to combat rumors.

Personnel Management
One by One – Together
(Condensed from U.S. Jaycees *Leadership Dynamics*)

Awareness –
Know each employee as a person.

Become aware of each employee's potential by identifying his or her strengths and weaknesses – to use each employee effectively.

Orientation –
Orient each employee to the organization and the team. Each one must know what is expected of him or her.

Outline the purpose of the organization, and provide a job description.

Relate to the Employee's Needs –
Show the relationship of the tasks to each employee's personal needs.

Make sure the employee feels confident in performing his or her tasks.

Help the Employee Grow –
Provide necessary training and guidance.

Help the employee establish his or her work and life goals.

(Experts have noted that more than 90 percent of the people don't really know where they are going or why.)

Build Team Spirit –
Outline the purpose of the organization, and provide a job description.

Make each employee proud to be on the team.

To make them proud of the team, you must first become proud of them.

Make Employees Feel important –
Send cards on special occasions – birthdays, anniversaries, holidays.

Ask the employee for suggestions and opinions. And then listen!

Ask employees to give reports to the team on their projects and work.

Send thank-you notes when he or she has done a good job.

Provide recognition through in-house publications.

Ask top management to congratulate the employee for work well done.

React pro-actively when he or she fails – as all of us have on occasion.

Discuss – in private – what the employee learned from the experience and what positive actions can be taken to prevent a similar occurrence.

Delegating Work

Don't Try to Micro-Manage

Many leaders have a tendency to want to do things themselves, often thinking that it is the quickest way to ensure the results they want.

That approach is counter-productive.

The more you delegate, the more time you have for management work.

Delegate Operating Work

Many leaders have a tendency to want to do things themselves, often thinking that it is the quickest way to ensure the results they want.

Operating work includes such activities as:

- Operating a machine
- Writing a report
- Calling people to remind them of a meeting
- Typing a letter

List and Plan Management Work

Management work includes:

- Scheduling
- Planning
- Organizing
- Directing
- Controlling

Always ask:

- Is this management or operating work?
- Who should be performing this task?
- Is training needed to prepare someone to do it?

The Rumor Mill

Rumors Develop From:

Anger – Fear – Distrust – Dislike –

Wishful Thinking – and Uncertainty

Rumors may contain some factual information; but often are inaccurate and contain half-truths, private interpretations and suspicions.

Rumors are spread by the "grapevine," through which information frequently is conveyed faster than official communication channels.

How to Combat Rumors

■ **The quicker the facts are shared ...**
               the quicker the rumor will die.

■ **A special announcement is most effective.**

The best way to "debunk" the rumor is to formally and immediately announce the correct information to as many people as possible.

■ **Honesty is required.**

When all the facts aren't yet known, those in authority need to say so. And then they must make every effort to report additional facts as they become available.

■ **Credibility is the best asset.**

The greatest asset a leader can possess to minimize rumors is credibility. Credibility does not automatically come with authority. Credibility is earned through respect and ethical actions.

(You lack credibility if you were misleading or had lied in the past.)

■ **Preventive action.**

Rumors can be effectively minimized on a continuing basis by a formal and frequent communications program.

■ **Use a periodical.**

A frequently published newsletter is an excellent tool to combat rumors.

WARNING: Some rumors, however, can be too damaging if too much time elapses before the next formal publication. A separate written and signed announcement may be necessary immediately.

10 – Problem Solving

The ability to solve complex problems is a skill highly sought in employees – and even more so in the selection of supervisors and managers.

It's a skill that leads to bonuses, better salaries and promotions.

The first step in solving a problem is drafting an accurate statement of the problem. That requires differentiating symptoms from the actual problem.

Problems usually are multi-faceted. That means each of the steps, parts, people, policies and locations involved must be researched, listed and examined individually.

In doing that, the main question to be asked is: What potential changes in any of those areas will help resolve the issue?

It might be considered a dissection process.

One solution process was outlined quite well in one of Louis L'Amour's books. In the following excerpt, L'Amour writes what his character is thinking:

"Long ago he had learned that problems could often be solved by that part of the mind that worked beneath the surface; that, given the elements of a problem, it was the nature of the mind to attempt to solve it, or at least to cope with it. The first essential was to see clearly what the problem was, to frame the problem correctly, and the means of solving it would often come without too much working at it."

That method can work often – but not always.

In seeking solutions to problems, we must consider the employer, the staff, patrons and ourselves. A problem seldom is resolved appropriately if a leader merely assigns an additional task to himself.

That falls into the error category of micro-managing.

Sometimes solutions come as cited by Louis L'Amour. But because that system does not always work, leaders must be willing to discuss problems with staff members or co-workers. That means exercising the trust and openness detailed in the chapter on leadership.

Leaders cannot expect themselves to magically pluck all of the answers out of the air. Sometimes their efforts yield only a vacuum.

Managers should not be perceived as weak if they seek suggestions and ideas from their staff. That can be the smartest approach leading to the best resolution. It usually leads to the most in-depth examination of all issues involved.

The article on successful bosses by Geoffrey James, cited in the leadership chapter, concluded with this observation:

"Successful bosses confronted problems by listening, considering options, deciding on the best approach, and then communicating what needed to be done."

I also like to cite two of the problem issues that I faced during my newspaper career as part of my management style. In those situations, the system noted by L'Amour worked for me.

That essay on Management Style is next, followed by guides on handling complaints and conflicts.

Management Style

(This article is reprinted from *Stories from The Golden Throne*.)

I worked under an editor who was an intimidator – but not for long.

And I worked under an editor who was a motivator. I enjoyed it; and I strived to develop a similar style.

Perhaps there is an irony in the fact that I was hired by the intimidator as a result of the recommendation by the motivator. Maybe it was because I was destined to see the contrast in the two.

The actions of the intimidator merely served to emphasize the importance of respect – respect for your staff members if you expect them to respect you.

I thought I was ready to take over the management of a newsroom until the motivator came into my life. Until then my conception of management included assigning, scheduling, technical training, monitoring, a bit of aloofness, budgeting and record keeping.

But from the motivator, I learned my conception of management responsibilities was far from complete – because it lacked proper consideration and emphasis on personal relationships and respect.

He taught me the importance of those two more by his examples than what he said.

He also advised me to complete three Jaycees programs in *Personal Dynamics*, *Leadership Dynamics* and *Time Management*. And I strongly recommend all of them to young folks beginning their careers.

My motivating editor often would leave little thank-you notes on the desks of different employees just to let them know that he appreciated our efforts in the day-to-day job of attempting to produce a good newspaper.

Such notes can have the effect of making a conscientious worker even more conscientious, assuming that's possible.

He also made it a point to recognize each staff member's birthday.

He would make assignments, explain the results he expected, provide training if needed, but otherwise simply allow the staff members the freedom to do the job without wasting his time looking over their shoulders or checking on them.

He explained:

"These folks are creative people. They know their job. Just tell them what you want, and when you want it; then let them do it," he advised.

He also recognized the need to shuffle the staff assignments occasionally – to end monotony and provide a somewhat different challenge for staff members who had been fulfilling similar assignments for several years.

He showed that he managed with the motto: "Praise in public; criticize in private."

I really don't recall whether he ever actually said it; but he lived it by his examples.

From him I also learned to always seek "win-win" solutions to problems. It's the "I win-you win" concept, rather than "I win, you lose."

Occasionally it's impossible when you have a staff member who simply fails to perform.

The best way, I guess, to emphasize the striving for win-win solutions is to cite two examples.

At the *Big Spring Herald* in west Texas, the publisher noted that the overtime in my department was beginning to climb a bit too much, and he asked me to examine ways to keep it under control.

116

Controlling overtime in a newsroom can be difficult. Obviously, seven-day newspapers need to have some folks working on the weekend, but newsrooms try to operate with a skeleton staff on weekends.

Naturally, unforeseen or unplanned-for events – whether on weekends or after normal shifts are completed – sometimes require calling one or more employees back to duty to handle the emergency.

Weekends especially were a problem in calling out a photographer or reporter after they already had 40 hours in for the week.

I had initiated a policy of comp time after the first evening call-out during the week, but overtime payment for the second call-out in one week. My staff members considered that a win-win situation. They liked having some time off during regular business hours to handle personal business.

That policy worked fine – except on the weekend when a worker already had 40 hours on the job prior to the first call-out.

The problem had me stumped – until I finally wondered whether it was appropriate and legal to begin and end the workweek at 5 p.m. Friday. So I checked with our business manager.

She said she knew of no legal reason, and could foresee no problem with her department's bookkeeping.

That moved weekend call-outs to the beginning of the work week, which made it easy to both control overtime and continue my comp-time policy for the initial call-out.

Another win-win success occurred shortly after I took over newsroom management duties at *The Daily Times* at Farmington, N.M.

The same two employees were serving as weekend editors every Saturday – one during the day, and the other at night.

When asked how long since they had a Saturday off, one replied it was nearly a year, and the other said it had been several months.

That situation is unacceptable, I said. I noted I would dislike a schedule like that, and that I will not expect anyone else to accept such a schedule.

I explained I was going to call in a third member of the staff to participate in working Saturdays. I said each of the three would serve in a rotation – with a month of Saturday days, a month of Saturday nights, and a month of Saturdays off.

I added that whoever is scheduled to work on a particular Saturday may switch with one of the other two – if both agree. But I emphasized that whoever was scheduled to work that particular shift is responsible for making sure that it was covered.

Those two men performed excellent work for me while I was with that newspaper.

Handling Complaints

Don't Try to Stop Complaints.

You have a better chance of trying to stop the sun from rising.
Instead, foster trust and positive relationships to reduce complaints.

Some Complaints Are Valid

Take action to correct the problem by eliminating the cause.
Quick action often avoids more destructive problems later.

A Checklist

Handle Complaints in Private

Have space available for private discussions.
Privacy provides for openness and a better exchange of information.

Put the Complaining Person at Ease

Note you are glad this issue had been brought to your attention.
Be sensitive to the fact that seldom is anyone eager to complain.
(Most people do so only when the annoyance has become greater than the dislike of complaining.)

Listen Intently

This is the most important item on the checklist.
Ask questions – tactfully -- to accurately identify the problem.
The issue may be a symptom of a larger, more significant problem.

Empathize with the Person

Show sensitivity to the person's feelings.

Repeat the Complaint

Summarize to show that you definitely understand the complaint.

Explain Action or Options Available

Ask about possible compromises.
Commit to giving a report on what you learn about the problem.

Don't Fail to Provide a Follow-up Report

Note you are glad this issue had been brought to your attention. Good relations result when they feel you are doing your best.
Failure to report destroys credibility and an opportunity to reverse a problem into a good public relations experience.

Dealing with Conflict

We all tend to shy away from dealing with conflict and confrontation, but managers and leaders usually do not have a choice.

Conflicts test a leader's ability

Potential Conflicts –

- Between team members
- Between the leader or manager and a team member
- Arising from leadership decisions
- Arising from overlapping responsibilities

Best Approaches –

- DO IT NOW!!!
  Waiting will only allow the problem to grow more difficult to resolve.
- Go Direct to the Sources.
- Follow Basic Rules for Dealing with people.
  - Be courteous
  - Listen to both sides
  - Recognize you could be wrong
  - Search for a compromise
  - Show no favoritism

Afterword

The Golden Throne Story

CB's – Citizens Band radios – were quite popular back in the 1970s.

They still are widely used by truck drivers, and still might be in some areas of the nation.

I occasionally went on camping and hunting outings with a small group of outdoorsmen, and frequently took my family camping when I lived in Utah for many years. Our group had CB's in our RV's.

I also remember that I wanted a distinctive "handle" – as our CB pseudonyms were called. I wanted a handle that no one else might use.

After my CB was installed in my pickup truck, I pondered different names for weeks. During that time, my family was going camping most weekends. And with a wife and daughters, we realized the need to acquire a porta-potty.

But when I priced them, I thought they were too expensive. So I decided to build one.

I bought a diaper pail with a lid. Then I made a box frame out of some scrap two-by-fours and plywood.

I took an old toilet seat and sawed a little off the sides and front to make it a bit square. Then I measured and mounted the toilet seat inside the box so that the seat would sit on top of the diaper pail lid and hold it in place when traveling.

And I fashioned a lid for the box out of some more scrap plywood.

I bought a can of school-bus-yellow spray paint and sprayed the box. I acquired a scrap of gold velvet velour material and a piece of 3- to 4-inch thick foam rubber. Then I covered the top of the lid with the gold material over the foam rubber to provide a soft seat.

121

The result was a disguised porta-potty that had the appearance of a hassock.

It was dubbed "The Golden Throne."

So guess what I chose for my distinctive CB handle?

Years later, when I was driving big trucks coast-to-coast, I started chatting on the CB to another truck driver as I was driving through Kansas. He asked for my handle, and I said:

"I bet you never heard a handle like mine before. I'm The Golden Throne."

He surprised me when he said, "Yeah, I heard that handle once before."

"When and where was that?" I asked.

"Wait a minute, let me think," he said. Then he added, "Oh, I remember. It was last fall – last September – up in Wyoming. I overheard a couple fellows talking, and that's what the one guy called himself."

"That was me," I said.

Not long after that, I purchased a custom made license plate. It is a silver license plate. But on the right side is a gold toilet – complete with water closet – inset on a red shield, with a dark blue sash diagonally across the shield.

It's my crest of arms.

In big gold letters on the left side of the license plate, it says *"The Golden Throne."* And at the bottom of the plate is the word **"Crusader"** – in honor of my years spent writing newspaper columns and editorials.

I keep that license plate in the aluminum brief case that I used when driving coast-to-coast.

Now you know why I decided to name my first book *"Stories from The Golden Throne."*

So this book has become another in *The Golden Throne* series.

Mystery philosopher known for many Western novels

(This essay originally appeared in *The Daily Times*, Farmington, New Mexico, on June 19, 1988.)

I like to call him the mystery philosopher – not because he isn't well known, but because few people think of him as a philosopher.

Many people have read some of his books – or at least heard of him. But probably few would call him a philosopher, because he appears to be writing mostly to entertain and provide us with a historical perspective.

Perhaps you've guessed that I won't tell you who this mystery philosopher is – until later, after I have established, beyond doubt I hope, that he deserves to be called a philosopher as well as a great writer.

A philosopher, by the way, is one who moralizes, who meets difficulties with calm composure, who expresses truisms and reports on the principles underlying conduct, thought and the nature of the universe.

My mystery philosopher does all these in his novels and short stories, which are based on historical and geographical facts.

He carries readers into some heavy subjects as his heroes exemplify high degrees of morality throughout his action-packed tales.

But enough explanation; I will let his writing convince you he deserves the title of philosopher. So here are some excerpts from his many books:

"Every boy wishes to be a man. One is eager to be given responsibility and to be worthy of it. So if you do your job and act the part, others accept you as you are. It is the willingness to accept responsibility, I think, that is the measure of a man."

* * *

"No man cuts himself free of old ties without regret; even scenes of hardship and sadness possess the warmth of familiarity, and within each of us there is a love for the known."

* * *

"… As far as the sea is concerned, you learn to live with the sea or you don't last. You simply try to conform."

"What about people? Do you conform there, too?"

"Whenever I can, of course. Why not? Most rules, whether of law or good breeding, are simply made to enable men to live together with less friction. If one lives with people he must always conform – to a degree. I see no harm in that, and lose nothing by it."

* * *

"What is education but a conditioning of the mind to a society and a way of life? There are many kinds of education, and often education closes as many doors as it opens, for to believe implies disbelief. One accepts one kind of belief but closes the mind to all that is, or seems to be, contradictory."

* * *

"Thinking was something I worked at like a prospector washing out gold. I'd take me a brainfull of the coarse gravel of ideas and sift it down until the gold remained. Only sometimes I worked a long time and came up with no color at all."

* * *

"Long ago he had learned that problems could often be solved by that part of the mind that worked beneath the surface; that, given the elements of a problem, it was the nature of the mind to attempt to solve it, or at least to cope with it. The first essential was to see clearly what the problem was, to frame the problem correctly, and the means of solving it would often come without too much working at it."

* * *

Note: This same problem-solving concept, mentioned only briefly by my mystery philosopher, is explained in detail in a book entitled "Psycho-Cybernetics" by Dr. Maxwell Maltz.

If you haven't peeked already, perhaps now is a good time to guess who my mystery philosopher is.

With one clue, it should be easy: He is the greatest Western writer of all time.

But here are a few more samples of his philosophy before I name him.

"Not that I deserved friends. I'd lived too much alone with a chip on my shoulder, always wanting friendship but wary of folks, fearful of what might come of trying friendship. Thing is, if a man wants friends he's got to be friendly. Takes a man a sight of time to learn the simplest things, it seems.

`"... To have friends a man has to be friendly, and to get others to think of you, you have to think of others ..."
* * *
"People often think of the law as restrictions, but it needn't be, unless it's carried to extremes. Laws can give us freedom, because they offer security from the cruel, the brutal, and the thieves of property.

"In every community – even in the wildest gangs and bands of outlaws – there is some kind of law, if only the fear of the leader. There has to be law, or there can be no growth, no security."

* * *

"Criminals suffered from two very serious faults. They believed everybody else was stupid, and the criminal himself was always optimistic as to his chances of success.

"The idea that men stole because they were poor or hungry was nonsense. Men or women stole because they wanted more, and wanted it without working for it. They stole to have money to flash around ... They stole because they wanted more faster."

* * *

"… Cops can make many mistakes; a crook need only make one."

* * *

"… I told her, 'You shouldn't waste time on me. I'm no good."

" 'If you think that,' she replied sharply, 'others will think it. Respect begins with self-respect."

* * *

"We are all on the way … A man is born beside the road to death. To die is not so much; it is inevitable. The journey is what matters, and what one does along the way. And it's not that he succeeds or fails, only that he has lived proudly, with honor and respect, then he can die proudly.

* * *

It's time to tell.

My mystery philosopher is Louis L'Amour, who died of lung cancer on June 9, 1988 – only 10 days before this essay was published.

I've read more than 100 of his books – many of them twice.

Several million copies of his books are in print – more than twice the number of any other American fiction writer. And many have been published in several other languages.

But because he's known mostly as a Western writer, he has received too little credit for the greatness of his writings.

I met him only once – in Ogden, Utah – and I have an autographed copy of the book "*Sackett's Land*." But I feel as if I have lost a friend as a result of his death.

This column was written before he died. Its publication, however, was delayed because of its length.

Most of these excerpts originally were presented as a speech at a Toastmasters chapter meeting. The objective was to report on one or more books dealing with philosophy, psychology or self-development.

At the risk of giving too much food for thought, isn't self-improvement often a matter of where we choose to find it?

# # #

Beauty and Life

(Originally published in *Stories from The Golden Throne.*)

I have kayaked the crystal clear lakes of New Hampshire and Montana;
Hiked the mountains of Utah, New Mexico and Pennsylvania;
Seen the beauty of desert flowers in Texas and California,
And looked down at my toes through chest-high salt water off the coast of
        Florida.

I have seen the sea of sparkling left by ice storms,
Coating weeds and trees in Oklahoma and Missouri;
Watched sailing craft catching the wind
Off Rhode Island, Maine and Puerto Rico;
And driven past the sapphire red of rosebud trees
Lining the interstate through Virginia and Tennessee.

I've watched the dawn rise over the shores of New Jersey and Maine;
Seen the sunsets from the peaks of Colorado and seaside hills of
        Washington;
Driven through snowstorms in Wyoming and Arizona,
And experienced the electrifying lightning shows across the night skies of
        western Kansas.

I've viewed Devil's Tower and the Grand Canyon;
Thrown snowballs in July in the Rockies;
Walked the edge of a mile-wide meteor crater;
Toured Yellowstone, Yosemite, the Smokies and the Everglades,
And snapped pictures of the bears and moose in Alaska.

I've seen whitetails slipping through the eastern hardwoods,
Enjoyed muleys feeding in mountain meadows;
Watched turkeys and elk sharing the same grove of aspens;
Chuckled at young raccoons devouring our camp scraps;
Rolled my eyes as a skunk came strolling under my lawn chair near a dying
        campfire,
And smiled at mama porcupine and her kits as they sauntered across the
        forest floor.

I've decided that tailored lawns and ruler-straight hedges of suburban
*   wealth*
Have nothing over the flaming orange and muted reds
Of an autumn mountainside in the Rockies,
Or the random multi-colors of October hillsides in the Appalachians.

I've absorbed the values bestowed upon me by honest and caring parents;
Learned to yearn for knowledge from the example of an older brother;
Experienced the passion and love of several good women
With fewer faults and flaws than my own,
And too often suffered the grief of family deaths.

Of course, there is much I have not seen or experienced;
But I have doubts that what I have missed can outshine what I already have
*   done.*
And through it all I have been blessed with good health and a sharing with
*   fine friends.*
But the greatest blessing of all was being born in this great country and into
*   a good family.*

So now I am savoring my retirement in Butte, Montana,
Where the pleasant disposition of the residents obviously is affected
By the wealth of sunshine the city receives – especially all winter;
And I will continue to enjoy as much more of this great life as my modest
*   means can provide.*

By Darrell Berkheimer – August, 2008